CW00322011

THE SIMPL

The Simplest Gift

STEFANOS XENAKIS

Translated by Thalia Bisticas

ONE PLACE. MANY STORIES

HQ
An imprint of HarperCollins*Publishers* Ltd
1 London Bridge Street
London SE1 9GF

www.harpercollins.co.uk

HarperCollins*Publishers*
Macken House, 39/40 Mayor Street Upper, Dublin 1, D01 C9W8

This edition 2024

1

First published in Great Britain by
HQ, an imprint of HarperCollins*Publishers* Ltd 2021

First published with the title *To Δώρο* in Greece by
Key Books 2018

Copyright © Stefanos Xenakis 2018
English translation copyright © Thalia Bisticas 2020

Stefanos Xenakis asserts the moral right to be
identified as the author of this work.
A catalogue record for this book is
available from the British Library.

PB ISBN: 978-0-00-845568-2
HB ISBN: 978-0-00-845565-1

This book is produced from independently certified FSC™ paper
to ensure responsible forest management.

For more information visit: www.harpercollins.co.uk/green

Printed and Bound in the UK using 100% Renewable Electricity
at CPI Group (UK) Ltd

For my father. My mentor and my hero.

CONTENTS

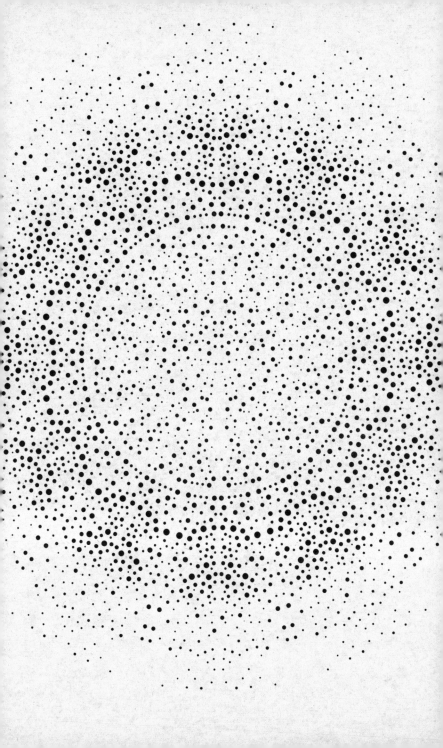

INTRODUCTION

I MUST HAVE BEEN IN THE FIFTH GRADE, but it feels like yesterday. I remember reading in my textbook that though most people can see, few observe the details of their surroundings. Back then, it didn't make much sense to me.

But I understood its meaning further down the line. I learned how to observe: to take snapshots with my eyes, but mostly with my soul. The snapshots I took were of things that many might consider trivial: a sunset, a flower, a smile, a nod. I began to find beauty everywhere. Even in the ugliness.

Along the way, I started to share the beauty that I found with others. I learned how to connect my life with the lives of other people, and in doing so I found we would become as one. That's when I realised that this was my true purpose in life.

I discovered I could take chances, face my fears, question my beliefs, and break out of my comfort zone. I learned how to escape the prison of my daily life. I had found freedom every day, every hour, and every minute.

I mastered how to hold my head up high, wear a smile, tell my own truth, say a good word, think before I speak, and work hard on my dreams. I realised that nothing would be served to me on a platter and that I had to earn my own life. Day by day, minute by minute.

A beloved uncle used to say that food only lasts as long as you keep it in your mouth. That's why you have to chew it well. If you swallow it, that's it. It's gone. The same goes for life. I learned to really taste life as though it was my mum's best home-cooked dinner. I learned to savour every moment.

Let me share with you a story that has always resonated with me. A farmer was digging in a field. At some point, his pickaxe struck something hard and it broke. The farmer was furious, and he bent over to see what had broken his axe. It was a box. He opened it and found treasure inside. Just like the farmer, I came to realise that I had to open life's boxes, even if I didn't like the wrapping. After all, in my experience some of the best gifts come in ugly wrapping. I learned that life itself is a gift.

Finally, I came to accept my missteps and mistakes. I learned to respect them, love them, and, along with them, love myself. That was the key for me. Instead of trying to make fewer mistakes, I let myself be free to make more. And because of this, I actually started to make fewer.

A decade ago, I began writing a notebook of miracles – my gratitude list. At first, I struggled to find anything to be grateful for, but soon I couldn't stop. Everything I saw was a miracle! The fact that I could speak, that I could walk, that I had a warm bed waiting for me at the end of a hard day. My perception of life had transformed; now I saw that life was overflowing with beauty. I realised that the beauty wasn't in what I saw, instead it was in my very own eyes. How I looked at the world determined the beauty I saw around me.

After that, I always kept my notebook with me. I wrote in it wherever I happened to be: at work, on the train, at home – everywhere! I filled the lines with precious words, the pages with wonderful miracles, and my bookshelf with countless notebooks.

And then, all of a sudden, something magical happened. One day, I stopped writing for me and started writing for those around me. I began sharing this wonderful thing spilling out of me.

The book you are holding is born of life.
My life. Our lives.

A few short tales and a lot of love.

I hope it helps to share with you the beauty all around us. Even if it only touches one person, this book was worth writing.

IT WAS WORTH ME ARRIVING HERE.

LILI

I WAS STARTLED. The phone doesn't often ring at 7 a.m. It's usually me who calls the girls to say good morning.

It was my eldest daughter on the line. She was sobbing. 'Daddy, Lili died. I found her dead in her cage this morning.' Lili was her bunny.

She sobs.

I paused for a long time before answering her:

'Avra, honey, how many years have we had Lili?'

'Not many, Daddy. Five or six.'

'Oh, Avra . . . That's how long bunnies live.' More sobs.

'From the moment we're born, sweetheart, the only sure thing is that one day we'll die.'

Everything begins only to end.

And everything ends only to begin again.

'Six years of Lili's life are at least a hundred human years. She had babies; she lived a happy life. She loved and was loved. Not many people have had a life as wonderful as Lili's, honey.'

Silence on the other end.

'We're all going to go one day, darling. Lili lived more than a hundred human years. How long do you plan on living? Two, three centuries?'

A hint of a giggle . . .

Children need to be aware of the facts of life from early on. They don't need to be cushioned from its realities. I took my father's shovel, picked up Lili in her box, and collected the girls after school.

'Hey, guys, do you want to bury Lili together?'

The youngest was thrilled with the idea. The eldest hesitated for a second or two and finally nodded. We went to our favourite hill near our house in Athens, where you can see the sea turn golden in the late afternoon.

We found a spot that wasn't too rocky and I dug a hole. I removed Lili from the box and wrapped her in tissue paper like a little bride. I took her in my arms so I could place her in the grave, but my eldest would have none of it. She pried Lili from me, like a mother taking her baby into her arms. She carefully unwrapped the tissue paper, brought her bunny up to her little face, and gave her a last kiss. She then gently placed her in the grave and put some lettuce leaves next to her, so she wouldn't go hungry.

'Close your eyes, my little Lili,' she cooed. She put some cyclamens next to her and we covered the grave before marking it with two big stones so we could remember where our beloved bunny was resting.

Then we went for ice cream.

'It's all part of life, girls. Everything is one. It's just us people that separate things into "good" and "bad". Rain and sunshine are one; life and death; love and fear; the sea and the mountain; the calm and the storm. Rain follows sunshine, winter follows summer, and bad times follow good. I used to like only the good stuff. Now I like both,' I told them, trying to sweeten the pill.

I didn't expect a response, but my youngest gave me the best one:

'SO, DADDY, YOU'RE SAYING THAT YOU LIKE WHAT YOU DON'T LIKE?'

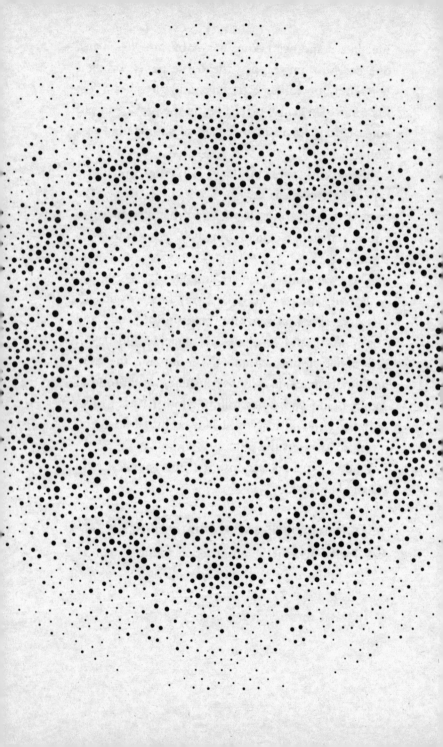

HONOUR YOUR PARENTS

HE'S A FRIEND OF MINE from Thessaloniki, tall guy – well over six foot. We used to eat out together every time he came to Athens. The two of us would go for a drink or two. Wine always helped coax out the truths.

On one occasion, we were joking around and my buddy was fondly reminiscing about his father. Then, all of a sudden, he started crying. Softly at first, then harder. In the end he was sobbing. I had no idea why he was crying, nor how to react. I didn't say anything for a while out of respect for my friend.

'Hey, buddy, what's the matter?' I finally asked him.

'My father . . . He passed away suddenly years ago. I was such a jerk and never told him how much I loved him. I only realised what a great guy he was after he'd gone.'

I just sat there with my friend, hurting alongside him.

We take so many things in life for granted. Our parents, too. Then one fine morning they slip away, and we are left with a load of stuff we wanted to tell them and never did.

If your parents are still alive, get up and go visit them. Today.

The universe isn't put on hold when your number is up.

Hug your parents.

Don't be afraid of hugging.

And tell them how much you love them. They've done so much for you.

Only if you have your own kids will you realise how much. And they did it without asking for anything in return.

All they want is for you to love them back. That's all.

And all you need to do is show them.

Their mistakes were made with the best intentions.

Forgive them.

Their parents made them, too.

And you'll make them with your children, if you have them.

And there will come a day – and I sure hope it does
   – when your children come and hug you as well.
To forgive you.
Love your parents, friends. The way you love your
   kids.

**FOR IF IT WEREN'T FOR YOUR PARENTS, YOUR KIDS
WOULDN'T EXIST.**

THE WAKE OF A SMILE

I ALWAYS GIVE RIGHT OF WAY WHEN I'M DRIVING. It's one of those small gestures that makes me happy. One morning, I was driving past the supermarket and a small car was about to exit the parking lot. I stopped. It took the driver a second or two to realise I was letting her out. She was around sixty years old, well-to-do, with a short, stylish haircut, and had both hands on the wheel. She smiled at me politely, and started to nose out into the traffic. Just before she got out onto the main road, she looked at me again. She turned her face towards me and smiled, this time bringing into play all the features of her face, perhaps of her whole being. It was one of those smiles that couldn't get any better. As the smile receded, she softly lowered her eyelids in gratitude. It was like a second wave breaking on the shore right after the first one: unexpected and much more intense. The lady left, but the wake of her smile continued to soothe my soul for a long time afterwards. It was hard to believe that a feeling like that could be so strong.

Half a day went by. At some point in the early evening, I had pulled over to the side of the road and was texting on my phone. Out of the corner of my eye I spotted a vehicle next to me. When the traffic light turned green, I noticed the driver looking at me intently as if asking for something. I realised he wanted to get out onto the street. But it was a tight squeeze. The driver had a big grin on his face. He had one of those instantly recognisable faces. I waved him through. He didn't expect it and a child-like smile lit up his face and mine, too. He looked at me knowingly, much like the kid in class did when he passed you the answers to the class quiz under the desk when you had lost all hope. It was an amazing smile. He even stuck his hand out the window to send me a little wave of thanks. A bit further down, the guy popped his head out the window and nodded to me again, repeatedly, with gratitude, as if the quiz results had just come out and we'd both passed. I teared up. It was as if those two wakes of a smile had become one – a big one, too big to describe.

I appreciate all the small joys in life.

It's like finding seashells
on the beach.
Each one a small piece of
treasure.

I bend over and pick them up, one by one. I have a secret box somewhere deep within my soul where I keep them. Over the years, I have collected quite a few. I don't care how much they're worth in money. Every day I become wealthier and happier.

IT'S THEIR TRUE WORTH THAT MAKES ME RICH.

YOUR PLOT OF LAND

YOU WERE GIVEN A PLOT OF LAND. You were told to tend it and were taught the basics: to plough it, water it, fertilise it, turn the soil, replenish it, and let it rest. To love it.

Some people listened and did as they were told. But they stopped there. They thought they knew everything and didn't take the time to learn more.

Some didn't even listen to what they were told. They did what they thought was best. They got impatient and, in fact, often did the opposite of what they were told. Their plots of land dried up and didn't produce any crops.

Others decided to learn more. They read books, asked questions, and listened. And they learned the most important lesson of all: that they didn't know anything. They decided to keep on learning for as long as they lived. And their lives changed, and they changed the lives of others, too. And their plots of land became Heaven on Earth.

Some blamed their misfortunes on not being given a plot of land by the beach, or complained that their plot was dry, or that those who'd found success and made it big only did so because they knew all the right people. Some tried to come up with a different system entirely: one that would take from the rich and give to the poor, instead of observing what the rich and successful did and trying to follow their example. These are the people who envy their neighbour's wealth – all they wish for is that their neighbour's plot dries up.

Some people can't stand the cold in winter; others can't stand the heat in summer. Some can't stand the cold or the heat. Some don't know what they want. And others just want not to want. They believe that if they don't like January, all they have to do is rip out the page from the calendar. And they ask other people to rip it out, too. But it's the one who doesn't try to avoid anything that you should keep your eye on.

January is a given, as are all months and all seasons. There's a time to sow and a time to reap; a time to water and a time to plant out. Respect the rules and tend to your own plot of land. If you spend your time looking at your neighbour's, you'll neglect your own. Your only job is to nurture what you've been given so that you can make it the best it can be. That's how the universe works. What doesn't grow withers and dies in the end.

The good farmer knows how to wait and how to have faith. But first and foremost, he knows *how* to sow. This is something he'll have learned by working hard and making mistakes. Your mistakes are your experience, and you need to learn from them. Whoever avoids failure also avoids success. Think of it like a ladder. And for every rung you don't step on firmly and confidently, you'll fall two rungs back. At first, you'll water your plot too much; you'll plant in the wrong season; you'll forget to prune; you'll overuse your field. You won't love it. You'll moan and groan and leave it unfenced.

Do not be afraid of failure, letting the days roll by. Do not let your life roll by.

Every day is a gift. Open it. Don't throw it away.

Beware of the easy life.
It's a slow and sure death.
Love your problems.
They'll take you a step further.
Welcome the hardships.

THE STRONGER THE WIND, THE HARDIER THE TREE

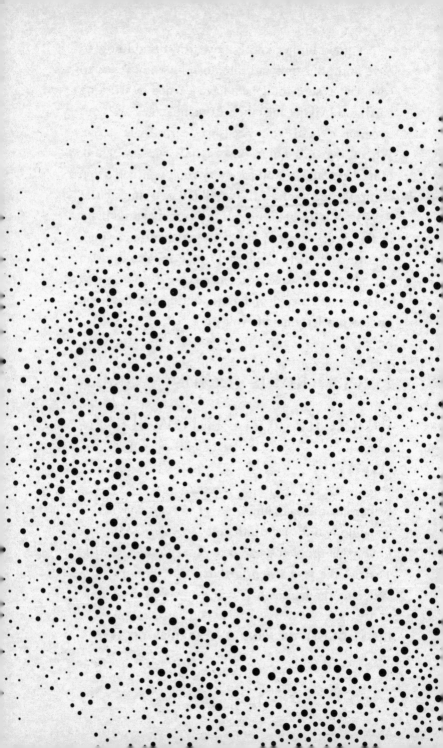

COME OUT SWINGING

YOU EITHER LIVE LIFE or it lives you. There is no in between. If the ball goes into the net, it doesn't come back. On one side of the playing field it's day, and on the other it's night. On one side, there's moaning and groaning, anger, helplessness, and depression; on the other, joy, sharing, self-worth, happiness, and strength. Of course, there are troubles on both sides of the field that you'll have for as long as you live. If your troubles are over, then it's all over. Some problems will make themselves obvious to you from the start. They're hefty and pumped up, reeking of sweat as if they've stumbled out of some second-rate gym. Others come disguised in pretty colours with a smiley face, as if they're winking at you.

I don't believe you can determine your future. But you do determine your habits, and they, in turn, determine your future. If you want to achieve what successful people have, then you have to do what they do.

Robin Sharma is a Canadian author and motivational speaker who has influenced me more than most. He taught me how important it is to wake up early. You should wake up, he says, at 5 a.m., when everyone else is still asleep and your energy levels are at their peak. Start your day by coming out swinging. Wake up in the company of your dreams, your goals, and get going with your morning workout. Wake up in the company of life. Plan each day as if you are the most important person in the world because for you, you are.

The most important message you send out by getting up early is the one you send to yourself. When you win the battle with your bed, you declare that you are in control of your life. The message is so loud that your other self will hear it, too – the couch potato, the idler, the snoozer, the one who nods to you saying you deserve to sleep in, the one who says, 'Why go out in the freezing cold?', the one who tells you to park your dreams a little longer until we're out of this slump, the one who has curled up purring next to the fireplace like a lazy cat. One self is on one side of the playing field and the other self is on the other. Get rid of that second self, the one who pulls up your dreams before they can even take root and steals your life before it can bloom. It's a slow death. Get rid of it.

Wake up and choose which team you're playing on.

The early wake-up call is the horn that blows at the start of the game.

BLOW THAT HORN. LOUD. SO THE WHOLE UNIVERSE CAN HEAR YOU.

WANT SOME GUM?

I GO TWICE A YEAR. He's my lawyer, and every now and then some interesting-looking characters drift in and out of his office.

On this particular day, I arrived on time. Makis is always swamped with work so you have to wait in a waiting room, like at the dentist. Some guy came in and sat down opposite me. I didn't pay him much attention. I just caught a glimpse of him out of the corner of my eye: goatee, smile, a kind-looking guy.

The secretary asked us if we would like some water. I said no. The other guy said yes. Him saying yes made me regret saying no. I smiled politely and he returned the smile. The ice had been cracked, if not quite broken. After a little while, he stuck his hand in his bag and glanced at me again.

'Want some gum?' he offered.

'No, thanks,' I answered quickly.

Then the 'dentist' invited me into his office, and I lost the guy. The meeting went well.

Later on, though, I recalled the man offering me

gum. It had marked my day. Like a single sunbeam through a cloud.

Trivial, you might think.

Sharing is never trivial. It's magical and powerful.

It's love in action. It's healing, most of all for the one who's doing the sharing.

What you share doesn't matter: whether it's a car or a book, the joy you feel is the same.

You either share or you don't. It's black or white. You either know how to play ball or you don't, but the good thing is that you can learn at any point. And once you've learned how to share, you can't live any other way. You get addicted.

You'll never discover the full potential of your day, your week, and, ultimately, your life if you don't say that 'thank you'; if you don't stop for that pedestrian or flash that smile at a stranger. How the other person responds is his or her own business: you stick to your business. But what you'll gain from making these gestures is magical. Your life will change. All of a sudden, you'll have what you've always desired.

John the Baptist said: 'Whoever has two tunics is to share with him who has none.' Now this is the important bit: you have to have two to be able to share. So make sure you do. Your car battery needs to be charged for you to be able to jump-start another one. Otherwise, you'll both end up with dead batteries.

There was a man named Joey Dunlop from Northern Ireland. He won the Formula One motorcycling world championship title five times in a row. Everyone adored him and he became a national hero – not for his gold medals, but for his heart of gold. The guy gave everything he had to underprivileged children. He'd buy food and load it onto his trailer and drive to Romania to give it to orphans there.

He was killed in an accident at the age of forty-eight. Fifty thousand people showed up to bow their heads to his greatness and celebrate his life.

Without a second thought I would swap a hundred years of a meaningless life for just an hour of a life like his. Don't just stare at your pack of gum, my friend. Share it.

THAT'S WHAT YOU'VE BEEN BROUGHT HERE FOR.

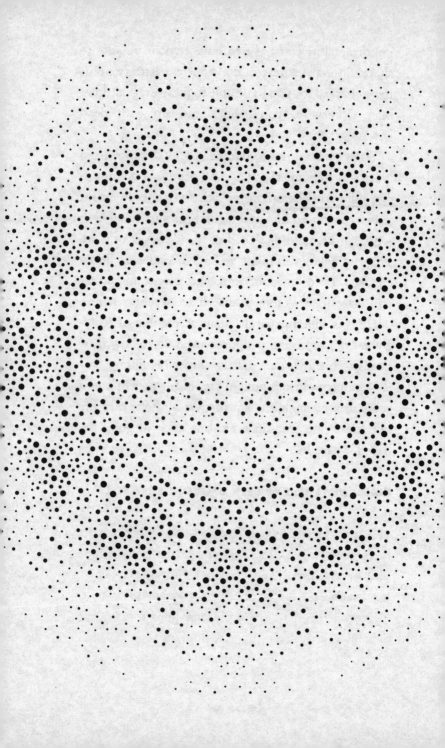

YOUR GOALS ARE
YOUR LIFE

NAVIGATING HAS NEVER BEEN my forte. I get lost easily. But for some time now I have had a GPS app on my mobile phone. Before starting out, I know where I want to go. I know my destination. If I don't know how to get there, I turn on my GPS. Sometimes, even if I do know how to get there, I still turn it on. It often shows me a better route. And in identifying a new route, I learn something.

Most people haven't determined their destination yet. They don't have goals. Some believe they do, but when they really think about it, they realise they don't.

A speaker asked the members of an audience what their goals were. One person raised his hand and said he wanted to make money. The speaker gave him a dollar. 'Happy now?' he asked with a smile. Your goal has to be specific and quantifiable. For example, I'll get down to 70 kilograms by next year.

We'll start having weekly family outings. I'll be making €100k a year in five years' time. Every April I'll have my health check-up. And so on.

A few decades ago, Harvard University involved some of its students in research to see how many of them had set goals in their lives. It turned out that only three per cent had. Thirty years later, the researchers looked up the participants of that study to see how they had fared. Those who had set goals had achieved, in financial terms, the equivalent of all the rest put together.

So, the more specific you are about your future, the more likely you are to make it happen. Goals bring the future into the present. They make the invisible visible. If you leave your life to chance, it just rolls along aimlessly. It can't follow coordinates if you haven't specified any. And at the eleventh hour, you can't turn around and say life was unfair to you. No, *you* were unfair to life. And to yourself.

You organise your weekend trips down to the last detail: what airline you're going to fly with, which hotel you're going to stay at, what sights you're going to see. But you treat your poor life like an unmade bed: each time you see it, you feel lousy, but you still don't make it. Your damn bed won't make itself!

Every person who has been wildly successful in what they do had a goal. And they were big ones. They wanted to change the world. And they knew exactly what they needed to change and how to do it. They set out their coordinates from the start. And then they got to work. Their dream was so vivid in their minds and hearts that, for them, it had come true long before it became apparent to anyone else. Look at Thomas Edison, Emmeline Pankhurst, Mahatma Gandhi, Martin Luther King, Rosa Parks, J. F. Kennedy, Nelson Mandela, and Steve Jobs, to name just a few.

Their dream was their compass. It was their life. Many of them would choose to sacrifice their lives over their dreams.

Helen Keller, an American disability rights activist, was asked what it was like not to be able to see. She replied:

'The only thing worse than being blind is having sight but no vision.'

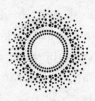

CRUELLA DE VIL

SUNDAY EVENING. I manage to squeeze in one last jog before the week ends. It's 8 p.m. and, as I'm driving back home from my run, I make a pit-stop at a café in a busy part of town to buy a bottle of cold water. I double park. The cashier is in plain sight, not ten yards from the car. Sure, double parking isn't exactly legal, but it's not going to put me behind bars for life either.

I'm just about to get out of my car when I sense someone's eyes boring into me. I turn and look. The window of the car I've parked next to is open. Hands on the wheel, the driver's giving me the death stare. Her gaze virtually drips poison. She says something I don't hear. I can feel her rage, but I don't respond. I remind myself that she's not mad at me; she's probably mad at herself. I start the engine and shift into reverse so I can let her out.

But the unthinkable happens: the car won't go into reverse. I try again. No go. This lady's mood has managed to curse the car, too! It's never done this before. I'm stunned. Now she's really furious, positively foaming at the mouth. She makes an abrupt manoeuvre to get out of her parking space. I kill the engine to give my car a breather and then restart it. It growls back to life, and I can finally get out of her way. She speeds off in true Cruella de Vil-style.

The old me might have picked a fight with her over her reaction. Not the new me. I now know how precious my energy is and I guard it with my life. I know how to tame my anger. I know that the confrontation with the driver wasn't personal. I know that nothing I could have said or done would have helped.

I now recognise what I can control and what I can't. I give my all to the things I can control. I make a detour around the things I can't.

My dad used to say: 'In one ear and out the other.'
Easier said than done, you might think. It's not; it
just takes practice.

I've since learned to steer clear of toxic people.
After this incident, my car never acted up again.

**MAYBE IT NEEDS A LITTLE PRACTICE STEERING
CLEAR OF TOXIC PEOPLE, TOO.**

ROOTS

EVERY SUMMER we go to the Greek island of Chios in the north-eastern Aegean Sea. It's where my family come from. As far back as I can remember, my parents made sure we visited often so we could keep connected with our roots. I fell in love with the place and now I take my kids there, too.

There's a wonderful routine to these trips. A couple of hours before the ship sets sail from the Port of Piraeus, a long line of cars forms. They're also taking families to the island. Friends reunite and newcomers are welcomed. There's much laughter and kidding around.

The next stop is the ship's cabin. The girls take the top bunks, making all kinds of enthusiastic plans about how they're going to bed down. They make little forts under the covers as if we're going to be staying there for days. The trip takes barely six hours. Then we go up on deck to wave goodbye to the harbour from the prow of the ship. We watch every step of the ferry's departure and Piraeus fading off into the distance.

In the restaurant we look for a table by the window. The stewards in their starched white shirts take our orders. I always get the rice with red sauce. That's what my dad always had, and he was a captain so he knew. Then we return to our cabin and tell stories in the moonlight. My daughters beg me for their favourites. I don't know who craves them most to be honest, me or them. They always fall asleep mid-story. I squeeze into the top bunk with my youngest on the inside, so she doesn't fall out, just like my mother used to do with me. At 4.30 a.m. the alarm clock rings. Still the dead of night. The steward knocks on the door to wake us for arrival. And they turn on the light, so we don't fall back asleep. I get up first so that I can wake them up in time and take them in my arms, just like my dad used to do.

Driving through the dark to the hotel, we pass by Myli, the three ancient windmills. My youngest daughter tells her sister, fast asleep beside her, all about the windmills. I can hardly contain my laughter. Further down is the statue of the Lost Sailor. This is where my favourite aunt used to take her strolls. Now she's strolling somewhere in Heaven and smiling down on our antics.

We arrive at the hotel. The little one is pushing her suitcase with one hand and rolling her scooter with the other. She refuses to leave it in the car. In the darkness, my daughter starts pushing her scooter with the fluorescent wheels round and round in figures of eight. Only she understands the importance of not leaving the scooter on its own. Only she feels the richness of her world.

We get to our rooms at around 5.30 a.m. The girls are in no mood to sleep. Nor was I at their age. The little one opens the fridge.

'Where are the sweets?' she wonders in disappointment.

'We'll get some tomorrow, when we go into town,' I reassure her.

I try to get them to go back to sleep. Pat-pat on their tummies and backs, a few stories. Before long, all three of us are fast asleep, sprawled one on top of the other.

Later in the morning, the eldest springs up. 'I'm going out to visit Grandma and Grandpa,' she says. I ask her for a kiss and she gives me a peck on the cheek.

All this has happened and we've only just set foot on the island!

That's the magic of having roots!
The magic of *living*!
Thanks, Mum and Dad.

Keeping connected to where you come from is a key ingredient for life. It makes me so pleased to be handing it down to my kids, in the hope they will do the same for theirs.

THANK YOU, BOTH.

COULD THINGS ACTUALLY BE OK?

I WOKE UP EARLY. I was in a warm bed with clean sheets. I got up and my legs held me up; they obeyed my every command. My feet took me to the bathroom. I turned on the tap and enjoyed the clean water gushing from it. I looked up and saw myself. Once again, the mirror was doing its job perfectly. I moved, and my image moved with me. I got into the shower and closed the glass door. The smell of soap filled my nostrils and I relished the hot water flowing over my skin for quite a while – words can't express how good it felt. Out of the shower, a warm, fluffy towel was waiting for me on the radiator. I wrapped myself in it.

I walked barefoot on the carpet to the window. I paused there. The raindrops on the outside were not coming in. I watched them slowly roll down and join each other in random patterns. I savoured this image for a little while. Then I picked out the clothes

I was going to wear. There were more clothes in the wardrobe, which I left there. I felt good.

I opened the fridge. A lot of options here, too. I made breakfast and squeezed three juicy oranges. The juicer worked its wonders as well. All I had to do was press the orange cup on the juicer head. I drank the juice down to the very last drop. I got ready to run some errands and left home, closing the front door behind me. Only my key will be able to magically open this door again. No other key can open it.

Now I walked to my car. Yes, I have a car that's all my own, which also opens with one unique key. I put the key in the ignition, turned it, and the engine started. I chose not to turn on the car stereo but I could have if I'd wanted to.

At lunchtime, I took a break, went to a diner, and ordered a tasty salad. While I waited for my order, I watched the people go by.

My eyes could see.
I was so incredibly lucky.

I saw faces: some happy and others not so happy. I saw people: some in a hurry and others taking their time. Wherever I looked, I saw shapes and colours.

My salad did not take long to arrive. It was served in a clean bowl with lots of crispy lettuce, warm chicken, crunchy croutons, and freshly grated cheese on top. It cost five euros. I had five euros. I took out my wallet and paid.

I also have a mobile phone. I sent some text messages, I connected to the internet, and I got updated on what was going on in the world. Facebook reminded me that it was a good friend's birthday. We hadn't talked in quite a while and so I called him. We were both glad to hear each other's voices.

I live in a beautiful, sunny country. We have peace. I know that tomorrow my house will still be there. No errant bomb will have razed it to the ground. We also have a democracy here. I can say whatever I want, wherever I want, and whenever I want. I can go out after 10 p.m. I can go for a jog, watch TV, take a walk, read a book, or waste time. I can see a friend or choose to be alone. I can smile. I can do whatever I please. I am the one who chooses.

In the evening, I returned home and unlocked my front door. The key did its job once more, without giving me a hard time. Yet again, my eyes could see, my legs could hold me up, and my hands could grasp things. My warm bed was where I left it. True, I hadn't solved all of my life's problems that day. Or solved world peace or the environmental crisis. But it was a beautiful day.

Maybe you don't have a house, a car, or a juicer. Maybe you don't have any money in your bank account and you're struggling to get by. No matter your circumstances, there are always things to be grateful for. That we are able to love, whether that be your parents, partners, friends, or children. That we can believe in what we want to believe in. That we woke up this morning, that we'll see a sunset this evening, that time will keep on moving. That you have a mind that is able to read and understand this very book. Even on the hardest days, we can still be grateful for the pain that we're feeling. Because without pain, it would be difficult to appreciate life's true joys.

HEY! COULD THINGS ACTUALLY BE OK?

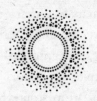

HUMOUR

LIFE IS A GAME: you only lose if you don't play. That's one of my mentor's favourite sayings. He told us this repeatedly until we got the message.

One day, while I'm waiting in line at the bank, I overhear an interesting conversation going on behind me and I start to listen in. A woman, probably in her forties, is talking to an elderly man. She's telling him how young her dad looks for his age. 'When people see us together, they think we're a couple!' she says. 'There he is! Dad, come over here, will you?'

I sneak a look. A cheerful older man with a spring in his step approaches. He's grinning from ear to ear, wearing Bermuda shorts, a trendy T-shirt, and a baseball cap – the eternal teen. He radiates energy. He's the kind of man you only need to look at to brighten your day. He jumps right into the conversation. 'How old do you think I am?' he asks the elderly man.

'Sixty?' wonders the man aloud.

'Seventy-five!' the 'teen' proudly declares. And he chuckles.

I turn around in amazement. I wouldn't miss the energy that this man is radiating for the world. I give up my place in the queue to the people behind me and worm my way into the conversation. The guy is one huge smile.

'Do I know you from somewhere?' he asks me. 'Maybe we go to the same barber?' and he chuckles again as he takes off his cap. There's not a hair on his head. Nor on mine. 'Do we go to the same dance class? Are you a winter swimmer?' The guy does it all. But first and foremost, he remembers to laugh. And joke. At every little thing.

Joy is everything. Laughter is the child of joy, and its parent, too – just like the chicken and egg story. When you're happy, you laugh, but you can also laugh to get happy. And underlying both is your sense of humour; it's what's in control of how you feel. Humour is life. It's the hope that something new, something special, is being born. Humour is the cele-bration of life.

People with a sense of humour are happier. They stay young. They get sick less often. They're shinier people – they glow. Wherever they go, they attract positive energy, as if they're sprinkling pixie dust around. They leave this world a better place than they found it.

A sense of humour is a sign of character, grace, and elegance. All the greats had one.

Winston Churchill and British MP Lady Astor were renowned for their witty repartees. Lady Astor once told him, 'If you were my husband, I'd poison your tea.' To which Churchill responded, 'Madam, if I were your husband, I'd drink it.'

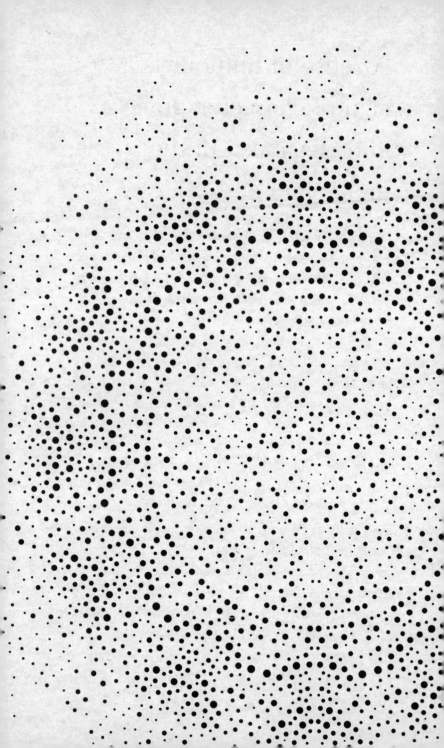

YOU CAN'T BE LOVED BY
EVERYONE

FACE IT. IT'S TRUE. It took me a long time to realise that you can't be loved by everyone.

It was 1 December, 1998. I was on stage, launching my new company. I was so happy I could have burst. And right at the best part of the presentation, this strange feeling came over me and the next second I couldn't utter a word. It was as if the power had suddenly been cut off: there was no sound. I opened and closed my mouth and nothing came out but air. Just like that, with no warning. Normally, the power might come back on after a few hours. But mine was cut off for six months. For six long months I couldn't articulate a single word. I could only whisper. Nobody could hear me. I couldn't even hear me. I almost went nuts.

Psychogenic aphonia they called it. The medical tests showed that my vocal cords were fine. The problem lay elsewhere. As is usually the case, it was all in my mind.

In the past, I had been the definition of the all-round 'good guy'. No one had ever said a negative word against me. Until, one day, somebody did.

A few months before I lost my voice, I was accused of something really bad – at least by my standards. And I couldn't prove them wrong. Eventually, after blowing off some steam, I thought I'd got it out of my system. But something was still eating away at me. I had become so worked up about it that a doctor friend later told me that if I had been older or not in such good health, I would likely have had a stroke.

From the time we are kids, we feel the need to seek other people's approval. We're taught to be good: clean our plates, obey our parents, and not cause trouble. In a nutshell, we're taught to pretend. As adults, it's hard for us to say 'no' to people, no to that favour they're asking. When you quiver at the thought of saying 'no', your inner five-year-old is pulling the strings. That child fears rejection and wants to make everyone smile and be happy. And the more those strings get pulled, the more they get into a tangled mess.

What's more important than pleasing everyone else is to be OK with yourself, to feel comfortable with that little voice inside your head that always knows best. You owe it to yourself to say those 'nos'. Your 'yeses' – the ones you say to yourself – should be the foundation on which your other choices firmly rest.

You can't be loved by everyone.
Once you come to terms with that it will change your life. You need to love yourself more than anyone else.
Only then will you be able to love others.

I recently heard the saying: 'I will take care of myself for you as long as you take care of yourself for me.' They used to call this selfishness.

NOW THEY CALL IT SELF-ESTEEM.

WATER GROOVES

A FRIEND OF MINE who knows all about farming explained to me what water grooves are. You dig a groove in the earth and at first the soil in the groove will be soft. As water passes through it, the soil gets wet and the water starts to mould the groove. Then, the water solidifies the groove. After that, it's as if your groove has been made from cement. The water recognises the path and follows it without thinking.

The human brain is made up of billions of neurons. Every time we have a thought or carry out an action, one neuron connects to another, creating a path. Each neuron can join hands with thousands of other neurons. But what tends to happen is that our neurons connect with the same neurons over and over again. It's called routine.

We take the same route to work. We wake up at the same time every morning. We watch the same programmes on TV. We think the same thoughts. We hang out with the same people. We make love in the same positions. We go on vacation to the same place. That's a treadmill, not a life.

The neurons in our brains are like those water grooves. The water has cemented them. Imagination, though, needs to run free. It needs to create, challenge ideas, and carve new paths. It needs to break free of routine. But we don't let it.

I jog every morning and, while I do, I like listening to an audiobook. I get through one every week. The other day, though, I decided to listen to some of my daughter's favourite music instead. I felt a little guilty at first, not learning something new, but then I began to enjoy the music. I returned home with a different sort of energy, mood, and mindset. I came back another man. I had cracked the cement.

Whether you think your cement is good or bad for you, the next time you find yourself succumbing to routine, try something new and see how you feel. If you run, take a rest. If you read, sit and do nothing for a while. If you cycle, take the car. If you like spaghetti, have some rice for a change.

Depriving yourself of what you like, even just once, is not a hardship. It's a strength.

The other day I shared an idea with a friend. 'Why didn't *I* think of that?' he groaned.

MAYBE IT WAS BECAUSE OF THE WATER GROOVES . . .

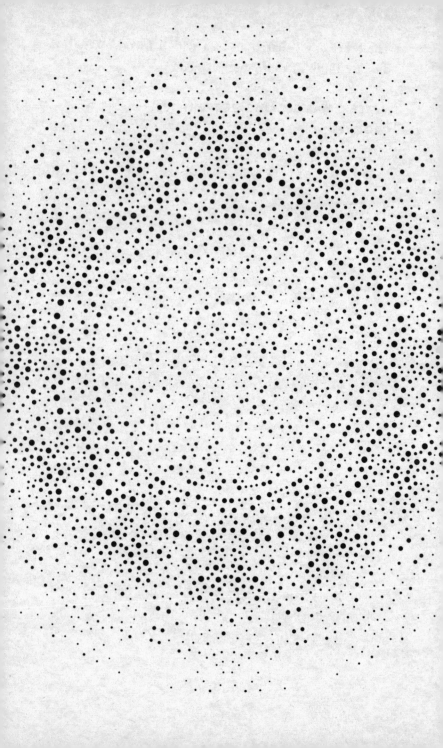

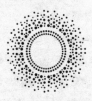

HOW MUCH IS A BOTTLE
OF WATER?

HOW MUCH IS A BOTTLE OF WATER? A couple of euros? Now, wait a second. At the supermarket you can get one for much less than that. But what if you're in the middle of the desert and dying of thirst? Then, you'd be happy to pay a fortune.

We were on our way home from the beautiful, small Greek island of Symi. We were taking the ferry to the larger island of Rhodes first, to get the plane from there. The boat ride lasts an hour and a half.

We went up on deck. At first glance, it seemed that all the bench seats were taken. But when we looked a little closer, we spotted one bench where a young man was sitting alone. 'Can we join you?' we asked. He nodded and picked up his backpack, which was next to him, even though we were going to sit opposite him.

We smiled a little awkwardly but didn't look at each other after that. Out of the corner of my eye I noticed another bag next to him. In a little while, its owner approached – his girlfriend. She flashed us a polite smile, too. We returned it without a word.

A little while later, we got up to make our way over to the stern to bid our farewells to the beautiful island. We gestured to the couple to ask if they could keep an eye on our bags. They nodded with a chuckle. Still no words.

The ship set sail and we returned to our seats. Our pantomime continued.

I went to get some water. When the steward asked me how many, instead of one, I said two. I hadn't planned to get water for the couple, but it just popped out. I like sharing.

When I got back to the table, I put one of the bottles of ice-cold water on the table in front of the young couple. They were pleasantly surprised. The girl thanked me and, all of a sudden, the ice and the silence were broken. We started talking about Symi, our vacations, and lots of other things besides. We were all happy.

We didn't become best buddies. We didn't exchange phone numbers. We didn't tell each other our life stories. We didn't have to, after all. But we made a connection, we felt good, we felt human. We shared smiles and it was wonderful. When we arrived at Rhodes, we exchanged heart-felt goodbyes.

It often takes so little to make someone happy.

How much did that bottle of water cost me? A couple of euros.

HOW MUCH WAS IT WORTH? THOUSANDS . . .

LESS IS MORE

EVERY TIME I WRITE SOMETHING I read it over and over again until I have edited out every unnecessary word. Getting rid of even one comma can be worth it. When you want to soar, you get rid of the dead weight. I used to try very hard to impress people by using lots of words. I thought the more I said, the more important I sounded.

Actually, often, the more you fear you don't know something, the more you say. And when you're confident in what you know, the less you feel the need to say. This realisation came as a shock to me.

The greatest speakers speak concisely. They go straight to the heart of things without detours.

Brevity is the source of wit.

The only thing the greatest teacher of all time said to his students was 'Follow me'. He didn't need to say anything more.

Simplicity and restraint can benefit other areas of our lives, too. In the past, my wardrobe was full of clothes. For some reason, I felt I just couldn't part with them. But one day, I decided to get rid of the clutter. My rule was that I would give away anything I hadn't worn for a year. My wardrobe and cupboards were emptier and my house could breathe. Everything felt calmer. I felt lighter.

In 2001, Steve Jobs asked his team designing the first iPod at Apple to make it so the user could play the song they wanted in just two pushes of a button. They insisted it could only be done in three. Jobs allowed them more time, risking the delay of the product launch. In the end, they achieved the two-push function. That one less press of the button made all the difference and was part of Apple's huge success.

A few years ago, I was at my favourite bookshop, looking for new books to read. One caught my eye and I only had to read the title to decide to buy it: *Less Is More*.

THAT SAYS IT ALL.

THE SIGNS

WE WERE IN A HURRY. We're always in a hurry when we're going to the amusement park. Neither the girls nor I want to miss even a minute of fun. They were in the back seat, goofing around and giggling. I was driving quickly, but not recklessly. And then a little red indicator light suddenly appeared on the dashboard. I'd never seen this red light before – but I quickly established that it had something to do with the tyre pressure. I tried to ignore it but I could still see it out of the corner of my eye. The nagging little voice inside me started to argue with me. 'Tomorrow,' I told it. 'No, today,' it responded. 'It might be serious. The petrol station is right there.' The car rolled into the petrol station as if on auto-pilot.

The attendant was as helpful as can be. I showed him the indicator. 'We'll fix that,' he told me. 'How much air pressure do your tyres need?'

'I don't know. Can you help me work that out?'

And he did just that. It turned out the pressure was too high. It was the spare I had put on the car last week. He carefully let out the right amount of air and I gave him a handsome tip. I used to be a stingy tipper. Not anymore. Tipping well makes me happy. The attendant flashed me a huge grin. We all smiled and got going again.

Maybe we got to the amusement park a few minutes later than we had planned, but I enjoyed our time there even more because I knew I had done what needed to be done. We often don't do the right thing. Instead, we do the easy thing.

We don't like pushing ourselves. That's why we don't lead the lives we want.

We ignore the signs – even if that little red light turns on. 'Why bother?' is the question that eats away at your life, little by little. 'Why bother to fix that tyre?' and then, 'Why bother to get off the couch?' 'Get that check-up?' 'Go to the gym?' 'Read that book?' And so the TV drones on, and you avoid those difficult conversations and you curl up on the couch. Before you know it, the years go by. And then you take a look at yourself in the mirror and you kick yourself because you let all that time pass.

At first, it's a little red light.
Then it's a huge, flashing neon sign.
And then it hits you over the head.
'Where the hell did my life go?' you ask.
'Who stole it from me?'
'My boss?'
'My partner?'
Take a good look in the mirror. You stole it.
And now it's time to give it back.
Time to notice the signs and do something.

GETTING TOO COMFORTABLE IS A SLOW AND TORTUROUS DEATH.

NONE OF YOUR BUSINESS

CONSIDERING THE WAY SOME OF US CARRY ON, I sometimes wonder how we manage to live as long as we do. The way we can get riled up about other people's affairs is enough to drive us to an early grave.

One morning, I was on my favourite pier at a beach near my home in Athens. I quickly said my good mornings to my fellow swimmers and got ready to dive in. And then I became aware of an interesting exchange happening nearby.

Two women in their early seventies, white hair, all skin and bones, were griping away to each other, like those two old geezers on *The Muppet Show*. I sidled up to eavesdrop. I don't miss chances like these.

'I'll tell him as soon as he gets out.'

'This has to stop. He did it yesterday, too.'

'Just look at her [his wife]. She hasn't even noticed. She couldn't care less.'

'If he drowns, it'll be her fault.'

'Typical!'

'He thinks he's invincible.'

'I'm telling him as soon as he comes out.'

'You do that.'

'There he is: he's coming out.'

I know the people that swim here, and I knew exactly who they were gossiping about. The guy came out of the water. He's in good shape, cheerful, and really likeable. He's in his seventies, too, but could easily pass for sixty. As he took off his swimming goggles, he sensed the pair lying in wait for him.

'How's it going, girls?' he asked with a smile.

'We're just fine and dandy, George, but you won't be if you keep carrying on like that,' one of them said, wagging a finger at him with her other hand on her hip.

From this point on, I don't remember exactly what was said, but the gist of it was: 'You take off your goggles and swim too far out. That won't do at your age. You're not a kid, George. What if something happens to you? What if you feel sick or get a cramp? What are you going to do then, huh?'

The more they went on, the more worked up they got. George just laughed. I dived into the water.

Granted, this is an exaggerated example, but we do versions of this all the time. We stick our nose into other people's business and judge them as if they've asked us for our advice. We think everyone should be more like us. We waste our energy and jeopardise our health for the sake of meddling in other people's lives. As if we didn't have enough problems of our own, we start getting on someone else's case!

Stick to your own business and let others stick to theirs.

When you're sticking your nose into other people's business, who's taking care of yours?

Nobody. That's who.

An incident from my childhood has stayed with me and feels relevant here. When I think of it, I don't know whether to laugh or cry. It involved two of my friends, Georgie and Nicky. Nicky had a strict upbringing.

We were at the beach and Georgie was just getting out of the water. For fun he put a sea urchin on his mother's leg, rather clumsily, and she was pricked by some of the needles. She screeched in pain, then scolded him, but forgave him pretty quickly.

Nicky asked Georgie's mother, 'Aren't you going to spank him?'

'No, Nicky. He didn't mean it.'

'Can I spank him for you?'

Pitiful.

AND YET, THAT'S WHAT WE DO.

SEE THE BEAUTY

I HAVE A DEAR COUSIN, a fine family man with high ideals who is good at his job. You'd have a hard time finding fault with him. But I did.

It's a beautiful spring day in April. The sun is shining brightly, but it's not too hot. My cousin and I, along with a couple of friends, are at a beach on the outskirts of Athens. Some people are strolling along the shoreline, while others are jogging or walking their dogs. Some people are swimming and some are playing racquetball. It's a celebration of life. Everything feels harmonious, like one of those model towns with miniature figurines where everything is so impossibly perfect. Well, on this day the scene was indeed perfect.

We were there for a couple of hours, having a great time – well, three of us were. Not the fourth. Guess who that was? The three of us had our eyes fixed on the beautiful blue sea and the surroundings. But not my cousin. We looked ahead; he looked back at the people laying out picnic blankets. We took in the waves and he saw the mayonnaise. He was so absorbed in the picnic that he was missing out on the scenery. And the more distracted he got, the more uptight he felt.

Focus can either breathe life into you or steal it away from you.

Success is having what you want.
But happiness is wanting what you have. Most of us don't get that second part.

We don't get it because we don't focus on the right things. We haven't realised how lucky we are to have two arms and two legs, a voice to be heard and ears to listen. We don't appreciate how lucky we are to live in a democracy where we can say what we please, when we please.

There's no such thing as objective reality. There's only subjective reality: each person is experiencing their own version of reality. They used to develop film in a dark room. That's where focus works. That's where you add colour or fade it out; that's where you brighten up the picture or darken it; that's where you make the image crisp or blurred. You could call focus a muscle – perhaps the most untoned one we have, but it's the most important of all. How you see the world around you will determine your happiness. It will determine your very life.

There were once two poor men who sold shoes. They travelled to a country where people went barefoot. One man left. 'They don't buy shoes here,' he said. The other stayed. 'This is where I will make my fortune,' he said.

AND SO HE DID.

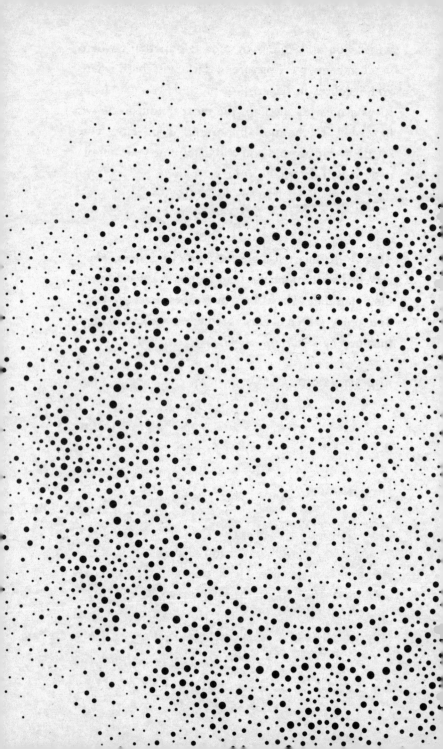

FIFTEEN HOURS TO VERIA

HER NAME IS IRENE. She's a language teacher and the kind of person who knows her own mind, stands up for what she wants, and gets the most out of life. Tactfulness and kindness are two more ingredients that make up this unique cocktail of a person.

She had contacted me and asked me to come up to the town of Veria, in northern Greece, to talk to the teachers and parents at the local school about a new class I've been designing. It's about teaching both children and adults to have a new outlook on life, and my dream is to get this class taught in all Greek schools.

The moment I set foot in the school playground I was blown away. This place took me straight back to my own school in Athens back in the 1970s: geophysical maps on the wall, blue-and-white school uniforms, water fountains lined up along the corridors, and kids playing tag. It was as if I had experienced all this in a past life. Except it was this life. The only difference was Lefteris, the smiling principal – the kind of principal I'd always wished I'd had.

About fifty teachers and parents arrived for the presentation that evening. They had a hundred reasons to stay home, spend time with their kids, enjoy their families, and relax. And yet, they chose to look at life from a different perspective so that they could offer their students and children a better tomorrow.

For two hours we were totally in sync. For two hours we poured our hearts out to each other. They participated, they asked questions, they challenged ideas, and they were inspired. At the end, they left with smiles on their faces, wondering: 'Could this magical life actually exist?'

Later, the teachers insisted on taking me out for dinner. Not at the expense of the school – they were paying out of their own pockets. I offered to pay my share, of course, but they insisted; these were people who had seen their pay cheques cut many times over in the last few years. They were proud people.

The next morning, I had to leave early, but I did manage to squeeze in a visit to the Veria Central Public Library. It's one of the few libraries in the world to win the Access to Learning Award from the Bill & Melinda Gates Foundation. It's the city's pride and joy, with 60 per cent of the city's population being registered members. Apart from books and DVDs, it hosts workshops, seminars, an inspiration room, theatrical performances and other events, 3D printers, and a recording studio. I was thrilled.

As I drove back to Athens, my mind kept going back to the educators I had met the previous day and the passion they had for making their vision a reality.

I'd invested a small portion of my life in theirs. And they had done the same – until we were of one mind. The most important lesson was not the one I had been trying to teach them, but the one they had taught me. About how wonderful it is to work with others and achieve something beautiful.

I am proud to live in my wonderful country.
I am proud to be Greek.

THE ELECTRICIAN

HE WAS RECOMMENDED to me by a friend of mine whose judgement I trust. Anyone this friend has ever recommended has turned out to be top-notch. Yannis was the name of the electrician and he was top-notch, too. I could tell as soon as he set foot in my house. He could be a scientist. In fact, he is, in his field of expertise.

Quick, precise, and neat. I went about my business and he his. He's the kind of person you don't have to tell what to do twice.

'This odd job needs to be done. Should I fix it?' he asked me at one point.

'Sure, fix it, Yannis,' I said, absorbed in my work.

'But to fix it, I need to break it first,' he replied.

'What was that, Yannis?' I said as if waking from a trance.

'To fix, I need to break, Stefanos. Can't be done otherwise.'

That got me thinking: to fix something, you often need to break it first.

My daughters do that when they play with their LEGO. They build castles, houses, and schools, and they love them. They don't want to lose them. But they run out of LEGO bricks to make new things. After moaning about it for a bit, they realise they have to break up the old to build the new.

I see it in life, too. Something dies to make way for the new; it dies in order to be reborn. This is true for relationships, friendships, businesses, buildings, emotions – everything.

We often get attached to the old. And yet, if we don't let it go, we can't make space for the new. There's no room. If you don't give away your old clothes, the new ones won't fit in your wardrobe. If summer doesn't pass, autumn won't come. If you don't empty your mind, it can't be filled with new thoughts. But we don't like change. We don't want to give away those shirts, we don't want summer to pass, and we don't want to empty our minds. And then we go and treat our eighteen-year-olds as if they were still children; we can't get over the fact that our girlfriend/boyfriend has moved on; we act as if it is still 2011, in Greece's 'golden age' when things were 'better'. We'd rather drag the anchor along the seabed than pull it up. No wonder we're always getting sick.

When you resist reality, guess who wins.

If we keep looking in the rear-view mirror when we're driving, instead of looking ahead, guess what'll happen.

From the moment you are born, there's only one thing for sure: one day you will die. And the person who fears death the most is the one who hasn't lived. So start living.

NOT TOMORROW. TODAY.

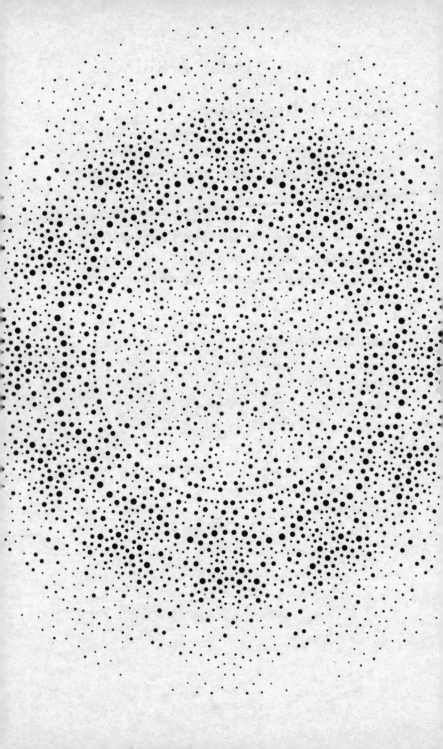

WAIT FOR KOSTAS

I WAS AT THE BANK. When we had finished with the paperwork, the courteous bank employee accompanied me to one of the two lines for the bank tellers. 'Wait in this line for Kostas,' she said. While I was waiting, I had time to observe the two tellers, Kostas and a woman. I soon realised why she had me wait for Kostas.

He was a young man in his thirties, wearing a freshly ironed, purple shirt. His hair was well groomed. His glasses complemented his eyes. He sat up straight in his chair and welcomed everyone with a smile. Though he was efficient at his job, he still took the time to say something nice to every customer. If his attitude had a message, it would be: 'The answer is yes. Now tell me what you need.' I continued to observe him as a woman approached with her six-year-old son. I waited to see if he would talk to the child. It was as if he had read my mind. 'How's it going, buddy?' he said and high-fived him with his eyes. The kid smiled and glanced up at his mum, beaming with pride. You'd think he'd grown ten inches in a second.

The other teller was a woman of about the same age as Kostas. But she looked older: her round glasses a little old-fashioned, her blouse slightly wrinkled, and she had a hunched-over posture. She wore a frown. Seeing them side by side brought to mind the story of Mr Smiley and Mrs Frown-face that I would read to my daughters. She wasn't bad at her job, but – how can I put it? – if you were a magnet, you'd be drawn to Kostas.

My turn came. I handed him the documents and explained what I needed. He got it right away. Two minutes later he'd given me a paper to sign.

'Is that it?' I asked him.

'Not so fast!' he answered with a smile. In another two minutes he had given me the rest of the papers. 'Now, we're done,' he said with a grin and then greeted the next person in line.

Kostas and the other teller make the same money. They work in the same bank and have the same boss. They live in the same country. But Kostas has found a reason to wake up every morning and go to bed with a smile.

It's pure joy to work with people like Kostas. It's even purer joy to *be* Kostas.

THIS TOO SHALL PASS

I HAVE A TUESDAY-MORNING RITUAL. My friend Mihalis and I meet at 6.45 a.m., just before sunrise. After our customary five minutes of small talk, we start running. Our run lasts for exactly thirty-five minutes. Our tongues get a workout, too, because we don't stop talking the whole time. Five minutes into the run we've already started going deep. We celebrate every victory because we appreciate that the little things are really the big things. Mihalis is a good man, an excellent professional, and a loving family man, who's rather hard on himself, if you ask me.

The runs always end with a dive into the sea. Today, Mihalis was in a rush so I went for a swim on my own.

I swam out to my usual spot and looked around to enjoy the view. I could see the apartment buildings lining the coast from afar. This image hasn't changed a bit in the last ten years. I can't get enough of it, even though I've seen it countless times; in the winter, in the summer, sometimes in the rain and even covered with snow.

Ten years ago, my company was doing really well and I swam to celebrate. Then, five years ago, it started experiencing difficulties and I swam to clear my mind. Two years ago, the skyline was the same, except one thing was missing: after years of struggling to keep my company afloat, I no longer had to worry about it. It seems like yesterday.

Time really does fly.

The *now* often seems like a vast ocean. Worries seem to flood you like a tsunami.

You think there is no way out. And yet, after only a year or two, as difficult as it may have felt at the time, everything will seem brighter. You'll realise that it all happened for a reason. There was some lesson to be learned there.

The King asked the Wise Man to share his most profound piece of wisdom. 'I'll give you half my kingdom if I have to,' he told him.

The Wise Man rejected the offer but gave the King a gift: a ring.

'Every morning, my king, you shall pick up the ring and read the inscription. Then, you shall put it back in its place.'

The King agreed. The next morning, he couldn't wait. He impatiently opened the ring and read what it said:

'THIS TOO SHALL PASS.'

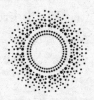

NEVER BE BEES

I T'S BEEN FIFTEEN YEARS, but I'll never forget this story. I heard it at a workshop.

The speaker took a deep breath. The expression on his face changed, as if he was about to share the secret to the meaning of life. And then he did. It was to become our secret, too, which we, in turn, would share.

'You place an empty bottle on its side by a window with the bottom flush against the glass,' he said. 'Sunlight comes in through the window. You put a bee in the bottle. The bee is a "smart" insect.' He stressed the word 'smart'.

'Bees have rules about everything – hard and fast rules, unfortunately. The bee knows that the exit is towards the light – no ifs or buts about it. So it'll keep on flying towards the bottom of the bottle and it will never get out. In a little while, it will die.'

'Now,' the speaker went on, 'put a fly in the bottle. The fly is a "stupid" insect. A fly doesn't follow rules. It knows that it doesn't know. And that's why it seeks to find answers. The fly will buzz around, up and down, left and right. In the end, it'll find its way out of the bottle. It will live. Never be bees,' he told us. 'And avoid other people who are bees. Always be flies. Know that you don't know, and keep seeking the answers.'

I see people shut themselves up in boxes – like those old, heavy iron safes. They put a combination on the padlock and lock themselves in. Somewhere along the way, they even forget the combination. And then they forget that they're locked up because the box has become their whole world. You talk to them and they don't listen. You show them the exit and they don't see it. They have become bees.

The problem is not what you don't know. The problem is that you think you know.

The more you think you know, the more you lock yourself in.

You've finished with school, but not with learning. Keep on learning until the day you die. Let knowledge in and bask in its light and warmth like you would in the morning sun. Immerse yourself in life. Don't let your days just roll by. Learn from them. Don't ask how much money you need to gain. Ask what you need to learn. That's the kind of life you deserve to live.

Socrates said, 'I know that I know nothing.'

ONE OF THE GREATEST MINDS THAT EVER LIVED WAS A FLY.

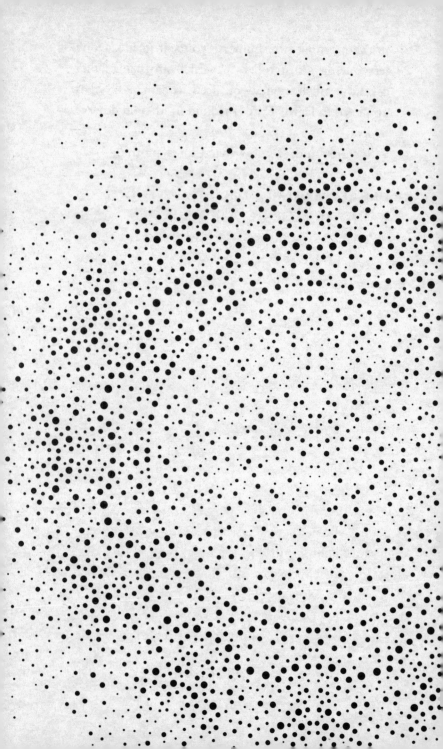

THE BEGGAR

THE FIRST TIME I SAW HIM coming towards my car, I avoided catching his eye. When he realised he'd get nothing from me, he tried the car behind. I peeked through the rear-view mirror to see if that car would give him something. Then the traffic light turned green.

The next time I saw him, I looked more closely. The hip knitted cap – the kind you'd never expect to see on a seventy-year-old – the grizzly beard, the bright eyes and the missing front tooth endeared me to him. When our eyes met, expecting nothing from me, he kept going. I got the feeling that he remembered me.

On our third meeting, I was a bit luckier: I had half a pizza on the passenger seat next to me. I had brought it with me precisely in case I saw him. As soon as I opened the car window, the man seemed to catch a whiff of it. I handed him the closed box, and that was it. His face lit up at once. His grin stretched from ear to ear and he was transformed, as if a time machine had taken him back thirty years, taking me along with him. It was like that gleam you see in movies when something magical happens. But this was no computer-generated effect. It was real and it shot through my whole being.

The next time I came across the guy, I didn't sense any expectation from him, and I liked that. He smiled at me from afar – pleasantly and on an equal standing. Then I remembered the bananas I had with me. I nodded to him and he hurried over. I offered him one. He grinned broadly in his now familiar way. It seemed as if he was thanking me for ensuring that he ate healthily.

Now we're pals. When I pull up at the stoplight near my neighbourhood, I search for him. When I have some food with me, I give it to him. When I have some change, I give him that. He recognises my car and when I approach that intersection, he looks for me – not persistently, but discreetly, the way he knows how. It's a relationship of mutual respect, where one does not depend on the other, where one appreciates the other's boundaries.

For some time now, I've learned to invest in relationships with strangers; people I meet for the first and perhaps last time in my life. A passer-by, the person at the toll booth, the cashier at the drugstore. A smile, a thank you, a good morning, a nod, all fill me with joy. It's as if my whole being is recharged, like the dynamo we used to have on our bicycles.

They say that what you give you get back. And it's true. It's like when you draw something on a piece of paper and that exact image is outlined on the reverse. But you need to give because you love to give, not because you're calculating what you'll get in return. If you don't, the image you draw will never be mirrored.

The bigger picture is a perfect balance sheet. The debit and credit always balance out.

It's like the accountancy course I took at university, where we learned that credit equals debit. The only difference is that you never know when your fiscal year is going to end and, in any case, you shouldn't care. The Great Accountant in the Sky balances it all out when he feels the time is right.

If your credit and debit don't balance out, don't complain. Add more to the debit side. But don't do it because you want your accounts in order. And don't expect anything in return. You'll get a return, but don't do it because of that. It ruins the formula.

You get it when you least expect it and from the place you least expect it. But you'll get it.

THERE'S NO DOUBT ABOUT IT. I KNOW FROM EXPERIENCE.

WHY?

IT HAPPENED ONE MONDAY MORNING. I was standing in line outside the bank just before 8 a.m. In front of me was a well-dressed, kind-looking, elderly lady with a cane. When the doors opened, we went in. The lady was third in line. Another lady further back had a good idea: that the people in front of her give the elderly lady their turn. The elderly lady thanked them but turned down the offer.

I told the lady that her suggestion was a good one and apologised for not having thought of it myself. 'You're right,' I said.

Her reply was sharp. 'I know I'm right, but what does it matter? She didn't listen to me.' She angrily returned to her place in the line, shaking her head and mumbling to herself. If she had been a cartoon, there would've been a black cloud hanging over her head. Her reaction seemed a strong one, but it didn't surprise me. I didn't respond. After all, she wasn't mad at me.

As I was leaving the bank, I became aware of the people around me. They all seemed gloomy and grumpy – as if they'd been affected by the event. It was like a parade of sad people. It struck me as strange, but I wasn't surprised about this either.

I walked alone for quite a while and a question came to mind. 'Why?' At first, it was a small 'why?' but it steadily got bigger and bigger until, at some point, this huge 'Why?' started to choke me.

Why don't we say 'please'?

Why don't we say 'thank you'? Why don't we smile?

Why are we afraid to love?

Why are we even more afraid to show it? Why don't we take care of ourselves?

Why do we feed ourselves worse food than our pets?

Why don't we service ourselves like we do our cars?

Why do we charge ourselves less than our phones?

Why do we badmouth ourselves?

Why do we waste our lives as if we're going to live for a million years? We only have 1,000 months. That's what it works out as.

Why don't we tell our problems to the people that caused them rather than tell everyone else and broadcast them on Facebook?

Why don't we delight in other people's joy?

Why is everything always someone else's fault?

Why do we always have some sob story to tell?

The other day I took a taxi home. Near my house there's an intersection without a STOP sign. I said to the cabbie, 'Careful here, because some people speed through.'

'They do nothing *but* speed around,' he grumbled. I bid him goodnight.

GIVE US A BREAK, PAL.

70 PARADISE ROAD

I'VE BEEN ON HOLIDAY WITH MY GIRLS for the past week on the Greek island of Sifnos. Yesterday, after our very full day drew to a close at a reasonable hour (for once!). It was a glorious evening so we decided to spend it walking along the beach.

The evening truly was magical, the kind you feel you can experience only in Greece: a starlit sky over a sea as smooth as glass. The waves broke on the shore just gently enough to sing you the melody of their music. The taverna lights twinkling in the distance, mirrored on the water, appeared like fireflies dancing on the waves. My daughters and I walked in single file as if we were the three Magi bearing gifts. We walked along that fine line where the sand was wet, but the waves didn't touch our feet. When a slightly bigger wave came along we'd leap, perfectly synchronised, to the side so we didn't get wet.

Soon, my youngest started wading into the water up to her ankles. That's where I bowed to the wisdom of nature. How different from each other we all are!

My eldest, the obeyer of rules, didn't get a single drop on her. My youngest, who has no time for rules, kept wading in deeper and we constantly had to reel her back in.

With one kid in the water and the other out, we continued to make our way along the shore, passing clusters of beach umbrellas. Some of them were fancier and more sophisticated, like well-dressed city folk sipping at cocktails and nibbling hors d'oeuvres at a classy restaurant, with elegant hands tucked in linen pockets. Other umbrellas were more off-beat, like laid-back bohemians – the non-conformists – the kind that can't stand their posh neighbours. And yet, they were all wonderful. Just as in life. Everything was perfectly harmonious, as long as the sense of harmony originated from you.

When there were no more umbrellas and the little ones started getting tired, the moaning and groaning began. But that was the moment when the magic really kicked in: fewer lights and more stars. There were a handful of blessed cottages arranged along the back of the beach. One of them, the smallest but the quaintest, had an illuminated sign. We went closer. It was a number: the number 70. It was numbered as if the house was on some busy urban street. We couldn't explain why it had a number, but, somehow, it fitted perfectly, like something out of an old, romantic song or part of a movie set that had been put up for precisely that purpose. Three women were sitting quietly on the porch outside the house overlooking the beach, enjoying the evening. I debated whether I should intrude, but I couldn't hold back in the end. 'You have the most beautiful home in the world!' I said, and they smiled.

We continued our walk. A young couple was taking an evening dip. Some kids were chasing each other on the shore. A little further down, a few groups of tourists were enjoying their evening meal in the last tavernas at the end of the beach. Everyone spoke in low tones, in keeping with the night calm. Everyone was in sync with this unique landscape.

We went on walking, telling stories under the billions of stars. I remember these stories from when I was a kid and even now they transport me to magical worlds. At times, the girls practically held their breath so they didn't miss a word. Keeping us company was that intoxicating scent of the sea and the sound of waves gently breaking.

On our way back, we stopped at the fancy umbrellas and ordered the girls' favourite virgin cocktails. I got a drink, too, and the three of us squeezed onto two deck chairs. The stories continued and, along with them, we shared secret plans and dreams. It was one of those evenings you hope will never end. The kind you know you'll never forget. The kind that makes you think that you wouldn't mind if your life came to a close like this. No exaggeration.

We finally returned to our hotel room tired but happy. We read a story about a king and a wizard and we all fell asleep, almost simultaneously.

It was an evening out of a dream, an evening in paradise.

It was as if that cottage had worked its magic on us.

THE COTTAGE AT 70 PARADISE ROAD.

TURN OFF THE TV

IT WAS IN 2001. I moved into a lovely apartment in the Athenian suburb of Vouliagmeni – quiet, overlooking the sea – just the place I needed to recharge my batteries and feel inspired.

My cable TV subscription had run out and it was time to renew it. Something inside me told me not to. And I listened.

For the first time in my life, I was alone without a TV, without that permanent, intrusive roommate that moves in without even asking.

For the first time in my life, I got rid of the remote, which had been the first thing I picked up in the morning and the last thing I put down at night. Things went quiet in my head. I found the solutions I was looking for. They were all inside me. The solutions to my problems had been knocking on my door all along, but how could I hear them over the racket of the TV?

For the first time since elementary school, I remembered what it meant to have free time. You hear people complaining that they don't have any. It's a lie. You have plenty of free time, but you throw it away at the end of the day.

Now there was no quick fix when I came home. So I went for walks. I called old friends. I sat with my thoughts, whether I wrote them down or not. I was, once again, the protagonist of my life.

The average person watches four hours of TV per day. The worst thing, though, is that they think it's free. Watching endless TV costs you millions. It costs you your dreams, your plans, your inspiration, your very life. One day, you'll wake up when you're eighty years old and you'll wonder where it went. You gave it away and you didn't even realise it. And now you're looking for it. But it's too late.

I have gained more than 10,000 hours since I stopped watching TV. That's more than 400 days. That's over one whole year – one year of solid gold.

If my suggestion seems too extreme for you, simply limit the hours you watch. Cutting down your viewing time by just one hour per day will give you 365 hours a year – that is nine working weeks. If there are twelve months in a year for everyone else, you'll have fourteen. Those two months are a gift to you and your dreams.

I remember when we first got colour TV in Greece. Around that time, I came across some graffiti with a message I'll never forget.

Colour TV. Black & white life.

WHOEVER THOUGHT OF THAT WAS WAY AHEAD OF THEIR TIME . . .

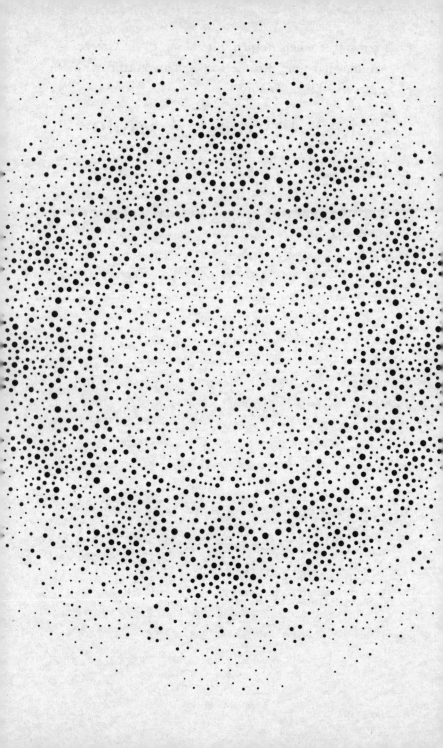

WHO ARE YOU?

THIS STORY IS TOUCHING AND TRUE and it happened in Tennessee in 1870. Ben had never met his father. Back then, it was considered a sin to be born out of wedlock and kids like that were branded bastards. Society was merciless. From the age of three, people would ask Ben who his father was, and Ben just bent his head in shame. The other kids wouldn't play with him. Mothers would steer their children clear of him. The older Ben got, the worse things became. School was a living hell. At recess he played all alone. At lunch he sat by himself. But weekends were even worse. When he went with his mother to the grocer's, grown-ups and children alike asked him the same question. 'So, who is your father?' And Ben bent his head even lower.

At church he was the last to enter and the first to leave, so that he could avoid the embarrassing questions. He felt like he was nothing. Sometimes he wished he had never been born. When Ben was eight, a new pastor came to his church. He was a lovely man, enlightened and kind, modern and open-minded – a true man of God. One Sunday, morning mass finished a bit earlier than usual and before Ben had time to slip away unnoticed, the pastor appeared next to him. He gently laid his hand on the boy's shoulder. To Ben's surprise, and to the amazement of the whole congregation, he asked him in a loud voice, 'Once and for all, who is your father, Ben?' It was so quiet you could hear a pin drop. Ben was on the verge of tears. 'Just a minute there!' the pastor cried out excitedly. 'I know who your father is! God is your father! And that is why you are so blessed! You have a great legacy, son. Go forth and do great things!' he told him.

The boy smiled. Tears streamed from his eyes, but this time they were tears of joy. For the first time in his life, he was someone. No one ever asked him about his father again. For the first time, Ben was proud of who he was – so proud, in fact, that he did, indeed, go on to do great things. Ben served two terms as the Governor of Tennessee. He was to go down in history as one of the most successful governors of the whole of the United States.

Ben had simply changed his identity. He was no longer a bastard. In an instant he had become a son of God. He was now the person he had always dreamed of being. It only takes an instant to change who you are, as long as you want it with all your heart. An instant is enough to be reborn.

Some of the greatest people who have ever lived experienced tormented childhoods. They were beaten or raped, or they were raised by drunkards. And yet, at some point, that magnificent moment came for them, too. *Their* moment. The moment they were reborn, the moment they got sick of the old and embraced the new. And then they nurtured this newness with care and diligence. And they became the people we all know.

And you? Who are you? Might you be the sob story you tell everyone? The one who wasn't able to study what you wanted? The one who had lousy parents? The one who's been hit by the recession? The one who doesn't like your job? Could you be the one killing your dreams? Could it be that your moment to become the person you have dreamed of has arrived? Could it be that your moment to be reborn is right here?

I'm with a friend and I'm telling him about my dream – the one about creating a self-awareness class and having it introduced to all the schools in my country. 'Dude,' he says, eyeing me doubtfully, 'you think *we* are going to change the world?'

'Yes, you jerk! *We* are going to change the world!

IF WE DON'T, WHO WILL?'

NOTEBOOK OF MIRACLES

I CAN'T BE OBJECTIVE about this. How could I be about something that saved me? Keeping a journal helped me transform my life. I've been writing in it religiously these last ten years. You could call it a journal of joy or a gratitude list.

I bought a nice notebook and started writing the beautiful things that happened to me each day. At first, I had a hard time thinking of anything to write down. When I opened it and the two of us were face to face, I felt strange. It was as if I was on a blind date and I didn't know what to say.

But I gradually started opening up. I wrote about a gorgeous sunrise. And about a good conversation. Scribble by scribble, I got something down on paper.

Ever tried tennis? It's just like that: if you keep at it, you get better day by day. Every day I wrote a bit more, slowly getting the hang of it. And I started realising how many countless beautiful things life had to offer that I hadn't noticed before. They'd always been there! It was *me* that had been absent. My notebook of miracles was to become my camera. I always carried it with me, taking snapshots of moments, and then developing them. But the greatest joy was when I put them in the 'album'. One by one, at the end of every day. Pure magic.

I started setting myself tasks. I decided I would write twenty things I was grateful for and I wrote twenty: that I got out of bed and my legs held me up, that I had water to enjoy a hot shower, that I had a warm bed waiting for me after a hard day. And so my life changed. Or rather, I changed.

I saw the beauty. In fact, I was staggered by the beauty.

My life continued to be what it was, but I now saw how magnificent life could be. And so my life became magnificent.

I've filled countless notebooks since that first one. I keep them on a shelf and re-read them sometimes. And I enjoy them just as much the second time round.

Some have called this practice conscious joy. And they're right. Instead of waiting for a delivery driver to ring my doorbell and bring me food, I get the pan out and cook for myself. When *I* want. With my own two hands. You could also call it home-cooked joy. It's the tastiest of all.

This morning, I stopped at the corner shop for a bottle of water. I opened the fridge and it was ice cold – the way you want it to be in the middle of a heatwave. I paid the cashier and said, 'What beautiful water you have, my friend!'

'You just made my day,' he answered with a smile.

'And you mine.'

HEY! LET ME NOTE THAT DOWN . . .

A WEEKEND AT THE HOLY MOUNTAIN

I'M NOT WHAT YOU'D CALL very religious, but I believe in God. In my own way.

Every spring for the past fifteen years, on Palm Sunday, I've been going on a retreat with a group of friends to Mount Athos (also known as the Holy Mountain) in northern Greece, home to twenty monasteries. It's something of a tradition for us and a chance to meet up. It's also our way of escaping the rat race for a couple of days, paying our respects, and enjoying ourselves.

A few days before visiting the monastery, you get in touch with the Pilgrims' Bureau to make your reservation. When you arrive in the town of Ouranoupoli, the 'gateway' to the Mount Athos peninsula, you obtain your visitor's permit for a small fee. A small ferry or speedboat, which are very punctual, will then take you to the monastic community. Upon arrival, you visit the *Archondariki* reception area and sign the visitor's log. There, you are welcomed by the *Archondaris* (the reception monk) and other monks with a warm smile, as well as a hot coffee and tasty Turkish delight, made even tastier after a long trip.

Mount Athos is a hive of activity. The monks buzz about like bees, constantly at work. They don't talk much and never complain. Though the buildings are made almost exclusively from natural materials, the monasteries and their surroundings develop at a dizzying rate from one year to the next. Everywhere you go, you see workers and monks hard at work, cooking, cleaning, cultivating the land, and building. They truly are a joy to watch.

The monks respect and honour nature. Nothing goes to waste. What the pilgrims don't eat, the monks finish off. And what the monks don't eat, the live-stock get. At every monastery you'll find cats and dogs that also live together calmly and harmoniously. The final leftovers become compost. Anything recy-clable is recycled. Some garbage is burned in a special kiln, so the final volume of garbage is minimal. You won't see a scrap of litter on the ground, of course.

Whatever the monks and pilgrims eat is almost exclusively grown on the premises. They buy only what is absolutely necessary. The monks till the land with respect and love. The food and wine are amazing.

Dinnertime is a sacred event. No one starts eating until the very last monk or pilgrim is seated in the dining room. That's when you'll hear the small gong that signals the start of the meal. We focus on the food set before us. No one watches television; no one plays with their tablet or checks messages on their phone. We eat with reverence. We honour the Creator. When the gong rings again, signalling the end of the meal, we rise in an orderly fashion and leave the room. Waiting for us at the exit is the Abbot, the first among equals, who blesses us. The Abbot always exits last.

Fasting is a way of life here and not restricted to the forty days of Lent. It means living and consuming with measure and respect for nature and other fellow humans, but most of all, for yourself.

Here, it's not just the Passions of Christ that are examined, but the passions of all of us. They symbolise our sins, but also the quirks of fate, our failures and missteps. We all make mistakes and we have the right to. Our mistakes are our experience. Here on Mount Athos, we are not ashamed of them. We don't sweep them under the rug. On the contrary, we shine a light on them.

That's why there's a second chance. It's called confession. It helps you acknowledge what you've done. You get it out; it makes you honest, first of all, with yourself. And you share your deepest secrets with the Wise Man. He's called a Spiritual Leader here and he gives you precious, heartfelt advice.

And then you get up and stand on your own two feet again. You're stronger, as if you've been reborn.

You see things from a different perspective – more optimistically. There's a Japanese saying that goes:

If you fall seven times, get back up eight times.

On Mount Athos it's called resurrection.

One day, I visited the gift shop at Mount Athos to buy some keepsakes to take back with me for my friends at home. Instead of a monk, I saw the Abbot at the cash register. This is the man that political leaders from Greece and all over the world come to visit. I politely asked him why he works at this post. He lowered his gaze and, as humble as could be, as if he was Christ himself, he said, 'To help out the priests, my son, who are busy at the monasteries.'

To me, this man is a true leader.

THE FIRST AMONG EQUALS.

EARS OF CORN

HER NAME IS SOPHIA AND SHE'S A KINDERGARTEN TEACHER. She found me through Facebook, and we arranged to meet and talk about the self-awareness class I'm preparing for schoolchildren. She's a genuine young woman, cheerful, dignified, and dedicated to her students. We agreed about everything until, in discussing her recent applications for a new job, we came to a sticky topic: do *we* ultimately determine our lives or does fate?

'I gave my all in the interview, Stefanos, but they didn't hire me at that school,' she told me. 'I was unlucky.'

'Did you do everything you possibly could, Sophia?'

'I did.'

'And if you were able to do it over, would you do it exactly the same way?'

'Well, maybe I would have done X.'

'Good.'

'And maybe Y.'

'Good.'

'So, if you did it again now, would you do it differently?'

'Probably . . .'

Do whatever you can in the now. Some things might not work out, at least not right this minute, but if you learn to give everything you have in the now, then maybe tomorrow those things *will* pan out. Do the very best you can at the given time. That's why you need to know more tomorrow than you do today. Keep learning. And take chances. Armed with knowledge and action, you are the one who determines your fate.

There were three men and each one was given an ear of corn. The first one ate it and his stomach was filled. The second planted the kernels and ten cornstalks grew. He had enough to eat for ten days. The third man planted the kernels, too, and ten cornstalks grew. But this man only ate the corn from one plant. He planted the kernels from the other nine cornstalks and ninety cornstalks grew. Again, he ate only one and gave another one to a friend because he knew about the beauty of sharing. He planted the kernels from the other eighty-eight cornstalks and 880 grew, and so on. Today, this man owns half the village and half the villagers work for him.

In the end, life isn't what happens to you, it is what you do with what life gives you.

More knowledge creates better options. And better options produce better results. Better results mean a better life. And that's what you want.
But to have better options you have to learn. In short: never stop learning.

KEEP ON LEARNING TILL YOU'RE PUSHING UP THE DAISIES.

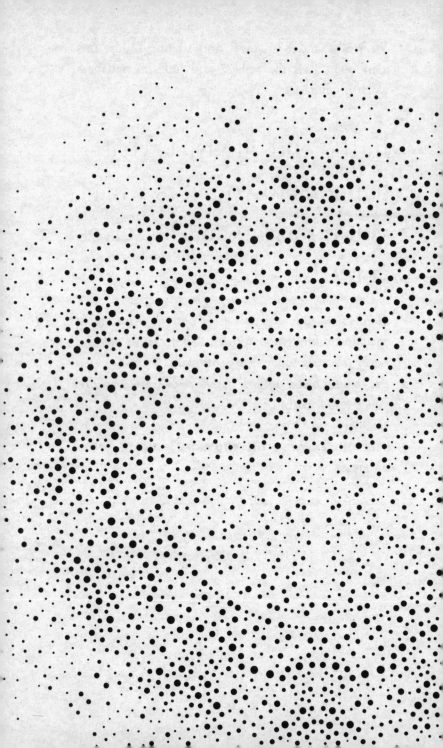

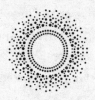

THE YOGA INSTRUCTOR

EVERY WEDNESDAY MORNING IS YOGA TIME. If I want something to happen, I have to schedule it in, otherwise, I know I won't get to it. A health issue led me to yoga and I've been practising for the past twenty years. That's how it usually goes: the most precious gifts often don't come in pretty wrappings with ribbons. That's why precious gifts can so often end up in the trash.

The practice of yoga has been around for thousands of years. It calms you, grounds you, elevates, and relaxes you. Nothing is left to chance in this unique philosophy of life.

We learn something new in every session. In today's class, the woman next to me didn't do a particular yoga position correctly, as we might say. I waited for our instructor's reaction – or rather, her lack of a reaction. I was right. She chose not to interfere so that my classmate could correct herself. She did. At the end of the class, we talked about it. We always talk about things like this and that's when the real lesson begins. Our instructor told us that correcting is not advisable. She wisely avoided using the word 'mistake'. (I heard somewhere that the word 'mistake' is a mistake in itself.) Any kind of correction or interference in someone else's life is, she concluded, a form of aggression – especially when it isn't asked for.

We often interfere in the lives of others: our children, our partners, and our co-workers. We have an opinion about everything, often without being adequately informed. We criticise and offer solutions without being asked. It's as if you're passing by your grocer and he stuffs a bag of bananas in your arms and then charges you for them.

At the end of the day, all people have their own goals, values, and priorities. Their own life.

I had this amazing experience a few years ago. It was evening and I was in a taxi on my way to the airport. I was content – it was during one of the easier times in my life. I was in the back seat doing my breathing exercises. The discreet cabbie didn't interrupt me. After a while, though, he couldn't help but comment, 'Man, I've been watching you in the rear-view mirror huffing and puffing. Who knows what you must be going through? You poor guy . . .'

I burst out laughing and then explained what I was doing. In the end, we were cracking up together. Even today, when I think back, I can't help laughing.

HOPE YOU'RE FINE, DUDE, WHEREVER YOU ARE.

HOW MUCH IS FIFTY EUROS?

I HAD PROMISED I'd get business cards for my daughters. They were nine and six at the time. I thought it would be a good idea so they could give them out to their friends, but also so they could learn about what it means to build your own identity and have goals. My daughters and I do stuff like that. One wanted to have 'Gym Teacher – Athlete' printed on her card; the other 'Gym Teacher – Explorer'. One wanted her card to be black; the other pistachio green – their favourite colours.

The printer calls me to tell me the cards are ready. I go to pick them up. They're perfect – exactly how the girls had imagined them.

Then, I pull out my wallet to pay for them. The printer tells me I gave her a down payment of a hundred euros. I distinctly remember giving her fifty. At first, I think: I'll keep my mouth shut. Fifty euros is a good sum. But then I think again. I'm not willing to sacrifice being honest for the sake of fifty euros. 'I gave you fifty, not a hundred,' I insist. She checks her notes and confirms that I'm right. She doesn't hide her surprise at my honesty as she thanks me.

Do I have fifty euros to blow? No. But I didn't blow it or waste it. I invested that money in myself, in my personal piggy bank, the one you can't see. This piggy bank is the most important of all because it's your identity and it's the most precious thing you possess.

Your identity is who you think you are.
And the person you become will always follow in the tracks of who you think you are.

You know? It's like your shadow. You'll never be able to go anywhere without your identity. And if you are true to your identity then it's the best feeling in the world. No money can buy that feeling. This is the feeling that will enable you to make your wildest dreams come true. It's an express train without any stops on the way.

I was walking on air when I left the printer's. I was my own person – the one that no one could buy off.

How much is fifty euros in terms of your self-worth?

ALL THE MONEY IN THE WORLD.

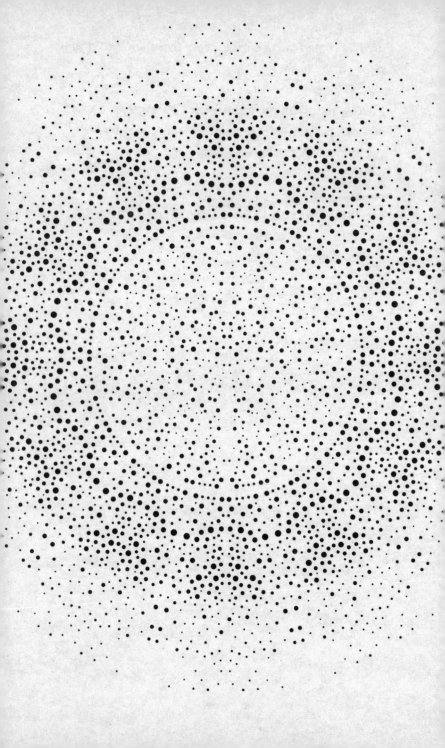

A GOOD WORD

I MOVED RECENTLY. The cleaner at my old place couldn't come to my new house so I asked a friend if he could suggest someone.

'I'll send you my cleaner,' he said. 'She's really good.' I spoke to her on the phone and she was available. We made an appointment and she got to work. From the outset I could tell she was responsible and thorough.

One day, I had to be somewhere else so I left her at the house to do her job. When I got back, she had already left. I had hardly shown her where anything was kept, but she had found everything herself: where the cleaning stuff was, where I kept the sheets and so on.

The house was neat as a pin. It was as if my fairy godmother had swept in and tidied everything with a flick of her wand. I was thrilled. In the past, I would have left it at that. But not anymore. I've learned to share.

I called her up. 'Hey, Valentina!' At first, she didn't recognise my voice. 'It's Stefanos.'

'Is something wrong?' she asked me anxiously.

'No, no. Everything's fine.'

'What is it?'

'I called to tell you that you did a great job. The house looks perfect,' I said, and added the fairy godmother comment.

She didn't answer for a few seconds. 'You mean . . . you're pleased?'

'Not just pleased. Overjoyed!'

She was stunned. Maybe she had never been spoken to like this. Maybe she was moved even.

'Thank you,' she said. 'Thank you very much.'

I could sense her smile coming through the phone. She was delighted. We arranged which day she would come the following week.

Say a good word.
First to yourself and then
to someone else.
They really need to
hear it.

More than you think. You will make their life better and, in turn, this will make the world better. Be generous with your praise. It'll bring more praise. Joy is to be shared.

It's wasted if you keep it to yourself.

I have a friend I used to work with who knows a lot about photography. I showed him a picture I had taken.

'Wow, Stephanos!' he says. 'Great photo!'

I was so proud to hear this I might have even grown an inch. 'Your framing is really nice. But you could have cropped it here.'

'Thanks, Nick.'

'And even better, you could have photographed the face like so.'

'Thanks, Nick.'

He made a few more observations.

'Thanks, Nick.'

He made a final comment.

'Dude, are you kidding? You've ripped it to shreds!'

I started laughing. So did he. But I listened to him. Because he had a good word to say.

BECAUSE HE MADE ME FEEL APPRECIATED.

APPRECIATE MONEY

I'VE ALWAYS BEEN GOOD with money. I made my first bit of cash at the age of five when my dad would get me to paint things on the ship where he was a captain. I put my first forty euros in my piggy bank. I'll never forget that feeling of having money you know you've earned.

Growing up, I always respected and appreciated money. And I taught my daughters to as well. They also made their first cash at the age of five. After school I'd sometimes take them to my office. They'd draw, type on the computer, make printouts, distribute papers, and do odd jobs. This is how they earned their allowance. They still have their first pay slip that they got from the accounting department with their five euros. They were bursting with pride.

In Greece, there are a lot of misconceptions about money: it's dirty, people who have a lot of it are mean, and the like. If you have prejudices like that, you'll never make money. Instead, we should talk about money as though she is a friend. She'll never stick around if you bad-mouth her.

Money is energy. It's neither good nor bad. It is whatever you are.

I heard somewhere about the 10-per-cent golden rule: invest 10 per cent of your income. It should never go in your pocket; you should deposit it straight into the bank or invest it. Live on 90 per cent and not 100 per cent. You might say, I can't even get by on 100 per cent; how will I manage on 90? Even if you make twice as much, you still won't have enough. If you don't invest it, you'll spend it all. Smart people invest first and spend second.

Don't grumble about money; learn its rules. Play with it. Play Monopoly with your family. Get your kids in on the game, too. Having money means having choices.

Every year before the Christmas holidays, my daughters sell handmade Christmas cards and they give a portion of what they make to charity. My friends often criticise this, saying that it's not right for children to work or that the cards are too expensive, and stuff like that. I just smile. And then I think back. If it wasn't for the money I earned when I was five and all the pocket change I got from doing chores when I was a kid, and learning how to handle money, I wouldn't have been able to write the book you are reading now.

IF YOU HAVE SILLY IDEAS ABOUT MONEY, GET RID OF THEM YESTERDAY. NOT TODAY.

THE GIFT

THERE ARE THESE FRIENDS of mine – the kind you make through your kids. The relationship starts like an offshoot of a tree, then it grows bigger and you can transplant it and it sprouts its own roots. It can grow into a tree, sometimes taller than the first tree. And so now you and the parents of your kids' friends have become better buddies than your kids were.

It had been a while since we'd met up so we arranged a play date for the kids, which was really just an excuse for us to get together. The mother sounded anxious on the phone and started telling me about her work. I cut her off. You don't eat a good meal on the run. You lay the table with the good china and enjoy it. The same goes for conversations – you should wait until you have the time and space to discuss things properly. 'We'll talk about it when you get here,' I told her.

They came over on Sunday. The girls went inside to play and we got right to the heart of the matter. My friend is very good at her job. I haven't seen her in action, but I don't have to. You can tell how good people are from the little things – even from the way they look at you.

It's a long story, but in a nutshell, my friend works for a large company, which values her contribution. And so does her boss. For some reason, though, a middle manager has come between them. This guy, according to my friend, has his own way of operating and you wouldn't exactly call him flexible. They soon clashed and he essentially assigned her the role of his sidekick. My friend complained to the senior boss, who sided with her. The three of them met together and the boss backed up my friend again, and the middle manager dropped out of favour. An important presentation to a big client was coming up and the middle manager split and left her in the lurch to do the presentation on her own. Thankfully, the presentation went very well.

My friend and her husband were really rattled throughout this conversation. The job has now become increasingly difficult and so has her day-to-day routine, they said.

But what I'd heard was a totally different story. And I started to laugh. 'Don't you get it?' I said.

'Get what?' she asked, all worked up.

'Hello?! The guy's warmed up his seat for you. From what I can tell, in a little while he'll be history and his position will be yours. A promotion. The new client will ask you to head the project. Would you have done the presentation if the other guy hadn't backed out?'

'No,' my friend said, somewhat puzzled.

'You should send him flowers.'

She thought about it for a moment. And then she turned to me with a big smile. 'I never thought of it like that.'

'And what if it *is* like that?'

What if life isn't what you think? What if gifts aren't in a pretty box tied up with a ribbon? What if some gifts come with thorns? You might get pricked by thorns when you pick a wild rose, but the fragrant blossom is your reward.

We often swim against the tides of life. The current pushes us downstream, but we swim upstream. We get exhausted and fed up and ultimately it makes us sick. And the ironic thing is that nothing you want is actually upstream anyway. It's all downstream. Sometimes, all you have to do is go with the flow.

Life isn't easy. But it *is* simple.

If you understand the rules, it gets easier.

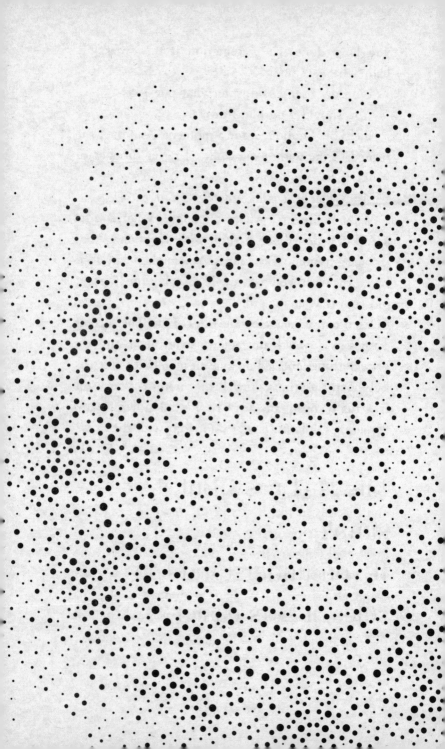

FIELD TRIP OF LIFE

THE GIRLS AND I HAVE been practising some of the same rituals ever since they were very little. It'd be easier to move a 10-tonne boulder than get them to change them. Every Friday morning, I take them to school. They call it a field trip. And this field trip has a bit of everything in it: laughing and teasing and singing, but most of all the excited anticipation of going on a trip. A typical trip to school goes something like this: we make a stop at their favourite pastry shop to get sweets. They race each other to see who gets there first. Each time we go, they try something new.

Then we pass by the church. There are stray cats and pigeons in the churchyard. They make sure to give each cat the same amount of breadcrumbs so they're all happy. They pet the cats, and every time they turn and look at me with this expression of wonderment and delight as if they've never done this before. Then, they play with the pigeons, which flutter around them as they scatter breadcrumbs.

Right after that, they go into the church to light a candle. They line up all the candles as if they're LEGO bricks. Sometimes they stick the warmed candles together to make one big one. They're always smiling, even when they kiss the icons and close their eyes to say their prayers. It's as if their smiles have been painted on their faces, with the kind of paint that doesn't wash off.

Then, they dash back to the car. More giggles, more teasing, back in field-trip mode. As soon as we pull up to the schoolyard, they want me to get out first so they can toss their schoolbags into my arms as if we're playing catch. Needless to say, it's a race to the classroom as well.

This summer we went on vacation to a hotel that had a huge swimming pool. It gets deep very quickly, so they came up with a game where they'd be merrily chatting away to each other in the shallow end when, suddenly, they'd slide down the steep bump and sink into the water. They must have done it more than a hundred times. They never got bored with it. They're always happy.

Children play no matter what they're doing. They smile and things are fun for them. They smile to make things fun. It's said that kids laugh three hundred times a day on average. For us adults it's fifteen.

We don't get old because we grow up. We get old because we stop laughing.

Children enjoy life.
They've discovered its meaning. They don't just exist.
They go on a field trip of life.

EVERY DAY.

THE PLASTIC BOTTLE

I MUST HAVE LEFT IT on my bedside table at some point. It was a plastic bottle with a little water left in it. For some reason, though, I hadn't got rid of it, maybe because I was too lazy, but probably for no real reason at all.

One morning, I decided to move it. Again, for no reason. I poured the water into a flowerpot and threw the bottle in the recycling bin. I'll never forget that day. Without exaggeration, it was one of the most successful days of my life. Whatever I put my mind to, happened; whatever I aimed for, I achieved. I had sent a strong message to myself – perhaps the strongest one I could: I determine my life, not luck. I control the strings. My life is my own. I live it; it doesn't live me.

What I'm going to tell you now is a true story. There was a famous speaker giving a talk to over a thousand people. At some point, he waves a hundred-dollar bill in the air and asks, 'Who wants it?' Many raise their hands. He asks again, 'Who wants it?' The rest of the members of the audience raise their hands, too. The third time he asks, one guy stands up, climbs up on stage, and snatches the bill from the speaker's hand. This is action. When the speaker asks the rest why they didn't come up to get it, they all have some excuse. One says he was sitting too far away. Another that he had to make the people sitting next to him stand up so he could get out. Yet another said she was too shy. We all have perfect excuses not to act. And the more intelligent you are, the more intelligent your excuses.

Action is about doing something, even if you're afraid or bored. Action is going against your very self when you have to. Action is doing the obvious. Not with words, but with deeds. Action is shutting your mouth when it would be easier to speak. Action is waking up earlier to organise your day. Action is giving your all at work even if you're not earning as much as you think you deserve. Action is taking care of yourself.

Action is living your life. Not just sitting and looking at it pass you by.

For you, action might be using that treadmill you have turned into a clothes horse, or making that phone call to a long-lost friend, or taking up that knitting project that's been collecting dust in the cupboard.

Whatever it is, start with something little. Start with the things that other people might consider unimportant.

If you want to change the world, start with that plastic bottle. You'll have won the first battle of the day. It'll make you proud and lead you on to the second and the third victory. It will help you realise that the small stuff is the big stuff. And if you can't handle the small stuff, then you'll never be able to handle the big stuff.

That plastic bottle is your boost for a better day.

THAT PLASTIC BOTTLE IS YOUR LIFE.

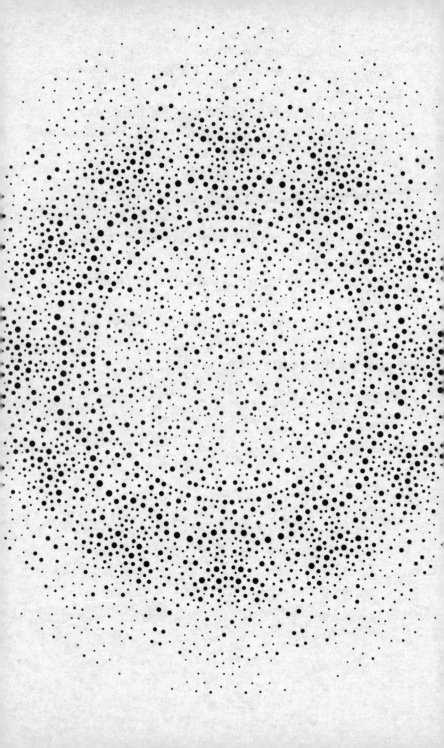

HAVE A NICE WEEK!

MONDAY MORNING. I'm stuck in traffic. The GPS says I'm going to be one to two minutes late. When I'm not at least ten minutes early to wherever I'm going, I get anxious, so right now I'm freaking out. And now I have all these street vendors trying to sell their trinkets or stuff pamphlets through my car window. So I go to close the window for a little peace.

And then I see her, striding towards me, like a cool breeze in the middle of a heat wave. I can't quite put my finger on what it is about her. I can't even see her face yet. As she approaches, I get a better look. She's wearing jeans and a freshly ironed shirt, with her hair neatly pulled back in a ponytail. She's tall, strong, and sturdily built – not what you would necessarily call pretty, at least not on the outside. But she has an amazing smile as she walks among the cars handing out leaflets.

My turn comes. She leans over to gently slip a piece of paper through my window. Her smile is even prettier than I had expected – warm and heartfelt.

That, too, slips into the car along with the leaflet. But she saves the best part for last. 'Have a great week!' she says. I sit there staring at her agape. It isn't *what* she says, but *how* she says it. You've made my week already, I think, but don't say.

You're not born a winner You become one.

It's not what you do, but how you do it. Success isn't the destination. Success is what you do on your way there. If you are driving on the motorway, success is every tunnel you pass through; it's your early-morning alarm, your coffee, your smile. Not the 'what' but the 'how'.

Drive like a winner. Keep your hands on the wheel. Stay in your lane. Use your indicator when you change lanes. But you're the one who determines your destination, and it should be non-negotiable. Whether you're a doctor, a teacher, or a rubbish collector, drive your life like a winner. Every single minute of your life. Like that young woman. I'll bet you anything she doesn't stay in that job very long. She's destined for better things.

IN FACT, SHE'S ALREADY DOING THINGS BETTER.

DOES LIFE HAVE RULES?

IT DOES. LIFE HAS RULES.

If you want to kid yourself and think it doesn't,
that's up to you.
But you can't boil spaghetti without water,
however much you try.

HUMANKIND'S GOAL IS HAPPINESS.

Happiness stems from within.
And when you share it, it multiplies.
It's a blessing to be able to delight in the happiness
of others.

LOOK AFTER YOURSELF.

Whatever you want to grow, tend to it.
Whatever you don't like, prune it.
You're the gardener of your life. Don't let
people tell you otherwise.

PEOPLE WHO ONLY LOOK OUT FOR NUMBER ONE WILL SUFFER.

Success is one thing and happiness
is quite another. Share.
Even with all the palaces in the world,
if you're bankrupt within, you're done for.

❊

YOU CAN'T FOOL YOURSELF.

Others, maybe.
But you can't hide from yourself.
You wake up together and go to bed together.

❊

LIFE ON EARTH IS BOTH HEAVEN AND HELL.

Life has a bit of everything. A friend once told me:
'In Hell, they have a pot full of food. But
the spoons are too long, so you can't eat.
In Heaven the spoons are long too. But there,
they use them to feed one another.'

❊

WHEN YOU AVOID FAILURE, YOU AVOID LIFE.

You don't learn how to ride a bike without falling
off. Your mistakes are your experience.

HARD WORK PAYS OFF.
You become an expert after a few thousand hours
of practice. Most give up after ten.
People who have what you want don't just have
connections, they buckle down and get to work.
Buckle down, too.

✺

THERE'S NO SUCH THING AS LUCK.
Luck is what you didn't do to get what you want.
It's what you left to chance.
Luck is just an excuse. Forget about luck.

✺

KEEP MOVING.
That's how the universe works whether you like it
or not. A bike either moves or falls over.
There's no such thing as an immobile bike.
The only way it stays up is with a stand. And if
you leave it for too long, it gets rusty.

✺

YOUR FAITH IS YOUR ROOTS.
You choose what you want to believe in.
Whether it's God, Mohammed, Buddha, or yourself.
Believe in something.
Otherwise, with the first gust of wind
you'll blow away.

YOUR OPINION IS NOT THE RULE.

If it isn't for you. That's the problem.
Learn to change your mind.

❋

YOUR LIFE IS YOUR RELATIONSHIP WITH YOUR SELF.

You will always carry your self within you.
If you are unhappy inside, you'll be unhappy
everywhere. Even in Heaven.

❋

MONEY MEANS OPTIONS.

If you're bad, you'll do harm with money.
If you're good, you'll create beautiful things with
money. Money isn't the problem.
Not having money isn't the problem.
Not having ideas is.

❋

LIFE DOESN'T OWE YOU ANYTHING.

Life isn't fair. Or rather, it is.
It won't give you what you need, or what
you hope for.
It'll give you what you lay claim to, what you
earn, what you conquer.

THE BIGGEST RISK IS NOT RISKING ANYTHING.

If you don't take risks, you're done for.
You've died but you don't know it.
Benjamin Franklin once said: 'Some die
at twenty-five and aren't buried until seventy-five.'

❋

YOU ARE THE ONLY ONE WHO CAN DETERMINE WHO YOU ARE.

Don't go trying to change others. Not even your
children. It's manipulation.
There's only one way of changing them.
Change yourself first.

❋

YOU REAP WHAT YOU SOW.

If you don't like what you're reaping, then
change what you sow.
You can't plant tomato seeds and harvest
cucumbers.

❋

PEOPLE ARE NOT TREES.

People move.
We let on we're moving on social media,
but we're not.
One moment is enough to change everything. As
long as you want it. And put in the work.

LIFE DOESN'T LAST FOREVER.

It lasts 1,000 months. Don't waste it.

YOU HAVE TWO EARS AND ONE MOUTH.

There's a reason for that.

YOUR CHILDREN DO NOT BELONG TO YOU.

They belong to themselves.
Catch on to that early enough and
you'll save a lifetime.
And theirs.

KEEP YOUR ANGER IN CHECK.

Your anger will kill you, not anyone else.
Confucius said:
'Before you embark on a journey of
revenge, dig two graves.'

YOU CAN'T STORE JOY AWAY.

It gets stale real fast.
You have to make it fresh every day.

YOU ARE THE STORY YOU TELL.

Change it and you'll change your life.
If you don't like the life you lead, create a new
story. You have the pen and the paper.

❋

YOU DETERMINE YOUR FORTUNE.

The same wind blows for everyone. What matters
is how you rig the sail. Rig it right.

❋

IF YOU DON'T ASK, YOU DON'T GET.

When you want something, ask for it.
When you have a complaint, make it.

❋

THE FURTHER YOU GO, THE LESS YOU KNOW.

One of the greatest philosophers that ever lived
said: 'I know that I know nothing.'
Socrates must've known a thing or two.

❋

LIVE IN THE NOW.

Only the now.
Be present in the now.
Yesterday and tomorrow are figments
of your imagination.

LIFE IS NOT A PHOTOCOPIER.
Don't imitate the lives of others.
Create your own.

❊

YOU GET WHAT YOU GIVE.
Sometimes it comes when you least expect it.
Life is like accounting.
It always balances out.

❊

FREEDOM IS YOUR OWN PERSONAL
AFFAIR.
Some are imprisoned in their wealth. But Mandela
was free in his cell.
You are the warden; you are the liberator.

❊

EVERY LONG JOURNEY BEGINS WITH
ONE STEP.
Take that step. Today, not tomorrow.

LOVE IS ALL THERE IS.

THE FIVE-EURO BILL

TUESDAYS AND THURSDAYS are my favourite days of the week. I pick the girls up from school and we do whatever we want. Every time it's something different – always a little bit surprising. My youngest gets out of school before her sister, so we sit and play games and make up riddles with her friends while we wait.

I had spotted him in the past. He was the school caretaker. Grey hair, clean-cut – a nice, hard-working guy. Anytime we had needed something, he'd been eager to help. But I didn't know his name and he didn't know mine.

The kids and I were kicking a ball around when he came up and asked me, 'Is this yours?'

'Sorry?'

'I found five euros. Is it yours?'

'No,' I replied automatically and continued playing.

'Right, I'll hand it in to the teacher's office,' he told me.

On realising what had just happened, I talked it

over with the girls. I tried to explain the nobility of this man. He was certainly no moneybags. He had a hundred reasons to pocket the cash. No one would have been the wiser. And yet, he chose to hand it in.

He did it for himself, so he could sleep at night, so his conscience would be at ease, so he could look the kids straight in the eye. I went and found him later.

'What's your name?'

'Spyros,' he answered guardedly.

'Congratulations, Spyros.'

'What for?' He was puzzled.

'For what you did.'

'What did I do?'

'For handing in the five euros.'

'But it wasn't mine.' Still puzzled.

These are the real heroes. These are the people who will teach us and our children core values for life.

SHARPEN YOUR SAW

I MET HIM IN SIXTH GRADE and he was to become my first mentor. He taught Greek. When I went to his house near the Port of Piraeus, I saw books everywhere – not an inch of wall to be seen. The books were like wallpaper – precious wallpaper. The whole house gave off that very special magical aroma that only a ton of books can produce. Many years later, I caught a whiff of this 'book smell' at the office of a friend of mine, a book agent, who had thousands of books. It took me straight back to that teacher's house.

This language teacher was to change my life. He tutored me in writing from the sixth grade until I finished high school. But these weren't lessons in essay writing; they were lessons in life. At the end of every school year, he suggested about a dozen wonderful books for summer reading. During those hot summer afternoons, in the coolness of my shuttered room with the scent of jasmine wafting through the window, I devoured those books. Every afternoon, I dove into their magic. Only the sound of my friends calling me to play ball could tear me away from them. For a while. Until the next afternoon.

As I got older, I continued to dive into the magical world of books. They were to become food for my soul. Even now, I'd rather feed my soul than fill my stomach. Of course, these days, books aren't only made of paper – you have ebooks and audiobooks, too. But even though these books don't have that special book smell, they will always be magical.

Every time you finish reading a book, you're not the same person as when you started it.

You're older, wiser, better. Books let your mind travel and expand. Books captivate you. They teach you to keep on learning until the last day of your life.

If you can read, but don't, you might as well be illiterate. Sadly, lots of people don't read. Somewhere along the way they stop learning; they stop evolving.

They race to and fro and get stressed out. You tell them, 'Hey, relax a little. Think. Change tack. Read. Get informed. Try new things. Take a step forward.'

'No time,' they say. No time, but they have time enough to watch TV.

So there's this lumberjack with his friend. The lumberjack is struggling to cut down a tree. Try as he might, the saw won't cut through the trunk. It's too blunt. But he just keeps sawing away for hours on end.

'Hey,' his friend says, 'you need to sharpen your saw.'

'No time,' says the lumberjack.

THERE'S ALWAYS TIME TO SHARPEN YOUR SAW . . .

LADY MUCK

I T'S A FEW YEARS AGO, and I am meeting a friend at a nice little restaurant in one of Athens's more affluent suburbs. I arrive ten minutes before my appointment, as I usually do. I sit down and start observing the people around me.

At the table next to me there's a woman of about fifty, one of those 'ladies who lunch'. She's sitting with her head in the air, looking completely aloof. The Brits have a name for snooty people like her: Lady Muck. She's dressed from head to toe in high-end designer clothes. Her outfit must have cost thousands. She is the kind of person who appears to care only about themselves, their house, their car, and, OK, about their kid.

An eighty-something-year-old lottery-ticket vendor enters – tall, thin, with a cane and a hump. He approaches Lady Muck's table. I know what's going to happen. I'm positive she's going to brush him off. I watch out of the corner of my eye.

To my utter amazement, though, Lady Muck

jumps to her feet to welcome him. She offers him a chair, pulling it out for him. The vendor is stunned. So am I. He sits. She pours him a glass of water. The old guy drinks it and thanks her. She then hands him the menu so he can order. He thanks her again, but hands it back. He's still at a complete loss. They say something, but I don't catch it. Then I spy him giving the lady some lottery tickets – a lot of lottery tickets. One by one, on and on. She must have bought half his tickets.

In the end, they both stand up. Lady Muck accompanies him a few steps to the door. The vendor is grinning from ear to ear, shaking his head in sheer disbelief as he exits. The lady is even happier.

I start laughing to keep from losing it. Now I'm ticked off at myself and not at the exquisite Lady Muck. But I've learned an extremely valuable lesson.

Don't judge.
Just watch and learn.

You see, judging and learning don't mix well.

LIKE OIL AND WATER.

FLUSH THE TOILET

THERE'S THIS RESTAURANT I'VE BEEN EATING AT for years. I still haven't decided if I keep going for the food, the ambience, or because it helps me think when I'm there. Maybe it's all of the above. What I know for sure is that dining with strangers makes me feel connected to them.

I often go and treat myself to a meal there. The food is always tasty and inexpensive. I always decide on the table I'm going to sit at and what I'm going to order on the spot. It depends on my mood and what there is to see.

Today, I decided to have stuffed vegetables, which begged for some feta. So I gave in and ordered that, too. I ate slowly, savouring each forkful. I looked around and felt peaceful. I listened to the inner me and felt calm wash over me.

When I was finished, I went to the men's room. The door was ajar. Someone was in there. A tall guy with a beard came out after a short while. He gave me a slightly embarrassed smile, and I smiled back.

I entered. He hadn't flushed the toilet. I didn't like this, and it set me thinking. I wondered how the rest of his day – maybe even the rest of his life – would have gone if he had flushed.

We live our lives on autopilot. We often don't even realise the consequences of what we do or don't do. And yet, we are our choices. Even the most insignificant ones.

Your life is what you do when you're alone. When nobody can see.

You can fool anyone. But not yourself. It's important to feel good about yourself deep inside: not on the surface of the lake, where the pebbles make little ripples, but on the bottom of the lake, where the pebble will ultimately fall.

Leave this world a better place than you found it. But first of all, make yourself a better person. Be the best person you can be. You see, those two things go hand in hand.

You might say, 'I can live without flushing the toilet.' And you're right. The thing is how *well* you'll live. For sure, you'll get somewhere. But where? If you want to cross the street, you're fine. But if you want to reach the top of the mountain, then you have to take that extra step. Make the extra effort. To reach the top of the mountain you have to reach the top of your own mountain, the one within you.

TO GET THERE, YOU'LL HAVE TO FLUSH THE TOILET, MY FRIEND.

BIRTHDAYS

I T'S LIKE LIVING IN A TRANCE. Like robots, we wake up, commute, work; we don't think, we don't feel. We exchange a few words, watch TV, and maybe a little social media to relax, and then off to bed. And there's the alarm clock again and it's back to the same old slog. But then there are those days when it seems we've been reborn, as if we're alive: birthdays, vacations, holidays, New Year's Eve. And, OK, when your favourite team wins the Superbowl.

And we all flood into the streets of Facebook – beep, beep! – traffic jams and cheering, happy faces in photos, wishes from all the friends, nice words . . . It's a celebration. But it only lasts a day and then it's gone, like a butterfly.

The moment the minute hand goes past midnight, it's back to the grind. Just like Cinderella – off with the glass slippers, on with the rags. Turn on the news, turn on the doom and gloom, and the long faces. And if it happens to be a cloudy day, it's even worse. It's like being in a funeral procession.

We learned back in school that there are 365 days in the year. But what we didn't learn is that every day is a gift. Every day is your birthday. Birthdays are in your heart and not on the calendar. Open the gift of each day and enjoy it.

You'll only realise what you've lost when it's too late – the joy you didn't experience, the love you didn't share, the gratitude you didn't feel, the beauty you didn't see, the good you didn't do.

Those things were always present, but you weren't. Only on your birthday and those other 'special' days did you knock on their door, and they eagerly opened to welcome you in.

There once was a wise prince in India. He understood that every day is a celebration. But he didn't want to forget it. So he had his servants remind him every day. Every morning when he woke up, he'd lie in a coffin and they would chant for him. After the ritual, he would climb out of the coffin and celebrate the day. He lived life. Every day.

Only when you are
nearing death will you
know what life means.

Start living your life every day.

AS IF IT WAS YOUR BIRTHDAY.

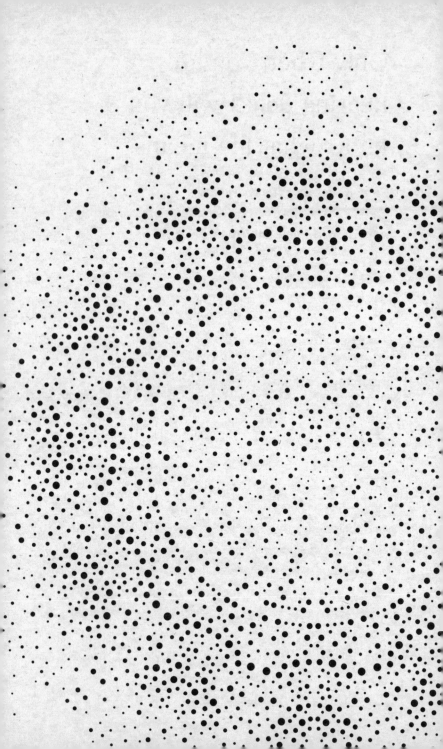

THE HAND OF GOD

I WAS OUTRAGED. I was pressing the buttons on my phone to send a text like firing rounds on the battlefield. Every letter was a gunshot. It was a long, insulting, and angry message. Very angry. I read it many times before I sent it, not so much to check it, but to savour it, a bit more each time. And then came the moment to press 'send'. I pressed the button. I had 4G and five full bars of reception. Guaranteed delivery.

For some reason, though, a little red icon appeared on my phone. The text hadn't been delivered after all.

I got ready to press the button again. My finger hovered over the send button, but this time I hesitated. The old me would have pressed it immediately and manically. But this time something inside told me not to. It was as if an invisible hand had caught hold of mine, giving me a chance to reconsider. This hand always appears at moments like these. And it's never wrong.

And so I reconsidered and thought about all the consequences. It would have been a huge mistake to send that text.

A word and a stone let go cannot be recalled.

If you send that text, you can't take it back even if you turn off your phone and take out the battery. A rocket has been launched.

I sat and thought about how immature and destructive it would have been to send that message. I would have forced the other person to answer. And there would have been no end to that war. Both of us would have lost. And any attempts to make peace the next day would have been futile.

And I thanked that invisible hand that had protected me. I don't know where it came from, but I promised to follow its advice in the future.

When I was little, my grandma used to tell me about the hand of God. This is what she must have meant.

HOW RIGHT YOU WERE, GRANDMA!

DON'T REACT. RESPOND.

YOU'RE PLAYING TENNIS. Your opponent serves you a fast ball. If you miss the ball, he gets the point. But you chase after it. You run all the way to the bleachers and manage to hit it at the last second. You send it back, harder, but with less control. Your opponent does the same. This shot is even faster. And so the volley continues. And so does the insanity of it all.

You're with your partner. They are irritated and say something foolish (as if you never have!). But instead of letting it go, you chase after the ball and send it back. They return it at once. At the end of the set, you're both exhausted and enraged. You don't want them in your sight. You don't want *you* in your sight.

Imagine the same story at the office, on the street, or at the bank.

In the well-known parable, Christ says to turn the other cheek. This is what he meant.

The old-timers used to say, 'Count to ten before you speak.'

I read somewhere that the word 'responsible' comes from the words 'able' and 'to respond'. People respond. Animals react.

There's a time to serve the ball and a time to respond; a time to let it go outside the lines and a time to return it. Sometimes you hit a volley and other times you hit it after it bounces, sometimes with more force and others with less, sometimes from the net and others from the middle of the court. And then comes the time to congratulate your opponent, the time to talk to them. And then there's the time to leave them be.

Learn to hit the ball right. Just like in life.

IF YOU WANT TO PLAY IN THE TOURNAMENT, THAT IS.

SUPERDAD

I DIDN'T NOTICE HIM as I was boarding the plane. I caught sight of him a little later when he turned around to see what his boys were doing. He turned his whole body, rather than just his head, to get a better look. It seemed a bit much to me, but kind of sweet.

He was in his forties, had greying hair and wore thin-frame glasses. He had that preppy look in a classic polo shirt with an upturned collar. There was a natural charm to his gaze, filled with love and warmth; just as much warmth as his kids needed – not too much and not too little. His gaze was also gentle, as gentle as a caress. It was as if every time he turned it towards his children, he didn't look at them but caressed them. With care and generosity, but most of all with respect.

It wasn't as if he wanted to check up on them or control them. He turned his attention to them and listened attentively, without annoying them and without invading their personal space. It was mostly them asking him questions, like you'd ask your mentor or someone you respect a great deal. And he listened to them, carefully, without interrupting or giving them an off-hand reply. He often seemed puzzled and wasn't afraid to show it. He'd look downwards to think for a moment. I observed him as discreetly as I could. Superdad had won me over.

At some point, he got up and passed by me. He smelled nice. He made his way towards the back of the plane after briefly leaning over his boys to see what they were up to. As he stood up, he gently ruffled their hair – again, not too much and not too little.

Then it was time for dinner to be served. The whole family had ordered the vegetarian option. Again, before starting his meal, he made sure his boys had everything they needed, like you would with an honoured guest in your home. One of the boys had noticed that the some of the other passengers were eating pasta. He asked his dad if he could have some, too, and with smiling eyes Superdad politely asked the attendant. She answered that they would have to wait until everyone had been served to see if there were any pasta dishes left over. Dad, in turn, explained this to his son, who was anxiously waiting. When the attendant reached the last rows, Superdad went to tactfully remind her, but there was no pasta left.

He returned to his seat and explained the situation to his son as if informing one of the most important passengers in first class. In the end, he gave him a tender peck on the cheek with his eyes closed as he held the boy's head with his other hand.

He wasn't what you'd call a typical dad. He seemed to have an invisible magnet that drew his children towards him. He had a magical touch and gaze. But even when he wasn't touching or looking at them, they appeared to be enveloped in an invisible cape of his protection.

You don't see fathers like that very often and I've come to the conclusion that we are responsible for that. We often fail to realise how important a parent's role is.

We try to force our children into our world instead of immersing ourselves in their magical world.

We often fail to treat them equally, but instead, pull rank, like you would in the army. We shout at them and don't listen to them. We are next to them but absent. We're lost in our own thoughts or our gadgets.

That day on the plane, Superdad reminded me that it's a big deal to be a parent.

SUPERDAD WITH THE UPTURNED COLLAR AND THE WARM EYES.

GOD BE WITH YOU

I SAW HIM OUT OF THE CORNER of my eye as I was driving round a bend in the road. Heavy-set, dirty, and exhausted from work, he was sitting on the stoop outside the factory. I was alone in the car and I pulled up to see if he needed a ride. When I'm on the islands, I often pick up pedestrians. They always have a story to tell, an experience to share, and a smile to give. I always come out a better man after my time with them.

'Where're you headed?' There was only one road on the island of Amorgos, so it almost didn't matter what he responded.

'To Kamari,' he said. He got in the passenger seat with some difficulty (a bit heavier than he looked. And more tired). He wasn't in the mood for chit-chat. How could he be after eight hours on his feet? The silence was broken by the ding-ding of the seat-belt warning.

'You have to put on your seat belt,' I said. He didn't respond. The ding-ding got louder. An awkward moment or two. After three or four minutes, it stopped ringing and there was silence again.

'Are you from around here?'

'Yes.'

'Do you live in Kamari?'

'Yes.'

'Are there many people on the island in the winter?' This got him talking. He told me about the 1,500 permanent inhabitants, about the school in the main town, and the bus that picks up the kids from all over the island to take them there. He told me about the recycling factory where he works. He managed to smile a couple of times, too.

Sharing is everything.

Open the door to let people in. Connect with people. This connection makes you a Human Being. Watch for that smile dawning on someone's face – especially the face of a stranger. It's as if the whole universe is dawning and the horizon is filling with colours. And so will your heart.

Neuroscience has now proven the kindness effect – what we used to call 'doing a good deed'. You need to care about the person next to you. Surprise that special someone, say a good word to a stranger, and help someone in need. All these acts of kindness produce dopamine, the hormone of well-being, happiness, and inspiration. You feel great about yourself and at one with your fellow humans, at one with yourself. You see, those two things go together.

So I listened to the likeable factory worker tell me about Amorgos until we got to his destination. I said goodbye. But he saved the best for last.

'God be with you, son!' he said and then closed the door and left.

I sat there watching him walk away with his bundle on his shoulder until he disappeared from sight. My eyes had teared up.

GRATITUDE.

THE DINER

I USUALLY GET REALLY HUNGRY at lunch-time. It wasn't even noon yet, but my car was already speeding me off to my favourite diner.

As I opened the worn, wooden door and entered, I noticed there weren't many people inside. The waiters smiled at me and I found a table next to the wall – the kind I like. I sat down and took in my surroundings.

Next to the window was a man of about fifty, bent over his soup in what seemed to be devotion. Completely oblivious to his surroundings, he gave the soup his full attention. Into it, he dipped his bread, his spoon, and his whole being.

A cheerful seventy-year-old in a youthful, bright red T-shirt with equally youthful features was sitting opposite me. The passage of time had drawn a perma-nent smile on his face – a genuine smile, the kind that brightens up the whole place. He knew all the waiters and had something to say to each of them. They buzzed around his table like bees around a hive. He didn't stop smiling at them as he ordered the lentil soup. It was as if he was going on his very first date.

After a while, two friends came in and sat at one of the front tables, which seemed to be their regular spot. They, too, were cheerful at the prospect of eating the tasty, home-style food that brought everyone to this diner. I was surprised to notice that the waiter served them two beers without even asking for their order – probably all part of their regular ritual. That's why I really like this place: it has five-star service that comes straight from the heart.

My food had arrived and, as I ate, I continued to observe my fellow diners. They all warmed my heart – all of them – from the guy diving into his soup, to the eternal teenager in the red shirt, to the two friends with the beers. It was as if they were all old friends.

Our tables were in a line, so I could take it all in. At some point, they all noticed me, too – except, of course, for the soup diver. We didn't exchange a word – only a few glances – but they were mean-ingful.

We dined together despite not knowing one another. It was like we were sitting at the same table, enjoying each forkful (or spoonful) the others ate. The soup diver left first. Then the two friends' order arrived with two more beers. The 'teenager's' lentil soup was almost finished, too.

I was the second to leave. Before opening the wooden door, I said goodbye to the waiters, and silently to my fellow diners. I may never see them again, but this small group of people warmed my heart that day. It was one of those moments you know you won't forget. I shot them one last glance through the window. A bit further down the road, the soup diver was waiting for the bus. I bade him a silent farewell, too, and headed towards my car. It was as if I had gone out to eat on my own and run into my friends.

Much like the friends you make on your journey through life.

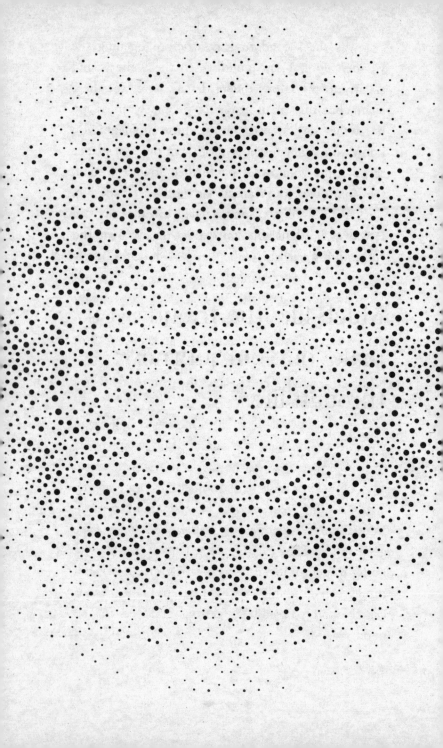

OWN GOAL

I LOVE VOULIAGMENI, especially in the wintertime. This Athenian seaside suburb gets a little less crowded then. And the colours change. It's as if the Big Boss is Photoshopping the picture: one day the sky is a bit greyer, the next, the sea a bit bluer, and the following, the wave caps a bit whiter. But this Photoshop software can also play with sounds, smells, and the wind, creating a different experience each time.

Sometimes people intrude on the image, but if you take them as a given, you can still enjoy it. Like lots of people, I used to get annoyed at any little intrusion. Now I just observe and sometimes contemplate.

It's a Sunday afternoon on the main street in Vouliagmeni. A couple has just parked and they're getting out of the car to go for a stroll. But they're going to get annoyed. Not that they mean to, but things can gradually become a habit and then a crutch, and you end up getting annoyed for no good reason.

The man gets out of the driver's seat, his face puckered with annoyance. 'Just get a load of where that arsehole parked,' he says, hissing his 's's. His girlfriend looks at the culprit and so do I. We're both puzzled. The car in front of him is parked slightly in front of the rubbish bin. OK, it wasn't the best parking job ever, but I've seen worse crimes. It wasn't as if it was blocking a garage exit or another car. I lingered for a bit to gather more clues, but that was the extent of it.

We spend too long with our noses in other people's business. The experts call it energy and it's the most important thing you possess. It's even more important than your health because your energy determines your health. There are things that we can control and that's where we need to direct all our energy. And yet, we often choose to waste our energy on things we can't control, usually by criticising and gossiping. And that's where we go wrong.

I walked on and thought about the couple. The guy had already ruined half his day and his girl-friend's, too. He had wasted his energy. And who knows how many times a day he does that? If he'd been a goalkeeper, he would have sent the ball into his own net.

There will come a moment when he looks in the mirror and says, 'Just get a load of that *arsehole*,' hissing his 's's again.

When we lack awareness, we fumble the ball.

By misdirecting our energy, we lose everything: our cheerfulness, our appetite, and our lives. And it's a damn shame.

THEY CALL IT AN 'OWN GOAL' IN FOOTBALL.

THE ART OF LIVING

I HAD ARRANGED TO PICK THEM both up in the evening to take them out. It wasn't my regular day, but after a while, when parents have split up, they usually find a few extra days in addition to the scheduled ones, to let the kids spend time with the other parent. That's how it was with us, too. The only difference was that my youngest had a stomach ache, so she didn't come this time.

So I picked up my eldest. When we're together during the school year, there's so much to do and so little time. In the summer, though, things are a little more relaxed.

We decided to go for a stroll in the seaside suburb of Glyfada. No plans, just go with the flow. When you're not with your kids every day, you learn to take advantage of every minute you're with them – every second even.

The shops were open, so we had a hard time parking. We decided to park in a car park. The first one was full and the second was going to close in an hour and a half, the same time as the shops. We likely wouldn't make it back in time before it closed. We soon figured out a plan: as soon as the attendant spotted a parking spot outside the car park, he'd park the car for us there and leave the key in our agreed hiding spot. I gave him my phone number so he could let me know where he'd parked it. After discussing it with my daughter, we gave him a handsome tip. That was our first success of the evening.

We made our way towards the cinema. I tried to talk her into going to see her latest obsession, *Wonder Woman*, the movie for grown-ups, so I could finally get to know this superhero. But she didn't want to, and I didn't push it. We continued on down the street for ice cream. In the quick debate about one scoop or two, I didn't have a hope in hell. We left with the large cones. Then we made our way to the park, which had been closed for months now. We considered jumping over the high fence like we had last time, but the park guard made us forget about that idea.

As we devoured our ice creams, we sought out our next adventure. The Glyfada school ground was a good place to find one. We went into the playground, where some boys were kicking a ball around. We exchanged a few passes, but it didn't last long. Following some other people into the school building, we could hear strains of music in the distance. It led us to a surprise: in a corner room there was a choir of middle-aged singers being led by their choirmaster. They were singing oldies, and we could also make out a violin in there. It was wonderful. We stood by the door to listen. At one point, the choirmaster shot us a glance but chose to ignore us. He continued with his work with absolute dedication. At last! This was the kind of thing we'd been looking for.

We left the school feeling revitalised and decided to get my daughter's scooter, which lives in the trunk of my car. We had another pleasant surprise awaiting us. Returning to the parking lot, we found the car parked in a space just outside. Two birds with one stone: we got both the car key and the scooter! Hurray!

We continued to wander aimlessly. I popped into a new store that stocked coffee and dried fruit and nuts. I tried some dried mango and apple and was so won over by it I bought two little bags to take home. My daughter wanted nothing to do with it. 'I don't eat dried fruit,' she cut me off before I even had time to offer her some. She gave me a coy smile and got back on her scooter.

On the downhill pavement, we picked up more speed than we should have and almost dragged two or three people along with us. Fortunately, all we got were looks from the pedestrians.

The next stop was a street seller who sold little handmade trinkets. My daughter spotted a pistachio-green pom-pom that cost two euros. Her little sister had been wanting one like hers and my eldest knew that pistachio-green was her favourite colour. As soon as she laid eyes on it, her face lit up. 'I'll put it by her bed so she'll find it first thing in the morning.' She climbed back on the scooter, whistling a happy tune.

We both had to pee by now and we spotted a sandwich shop further down where we could go. We bought a bottle of cold water and asked to use the bathroom. We wondered about the man ahead of us in the queue, who washed his hands *before* entering the men's room, but we drew no conclusions.

Then we had the idea to go to one of her favourite shops, owned by a hobbyist who sells rare LEGO pieces. I knew that taking her there could cost me a small fortune, but I agreed because I knew it was near closing time. He was just locking up when we got there. 'Oh, what a pity!' I said.

She gave me a knowing smile and replied, 'That's OK. We'll go to the big toy store with the escalators.' We picked up our pace to make it there before it closed. Here, I knew I'd be out of luck because they closed later, at 9 p.m. We got there in the nick of time and went straight to the LEGO section. We admired a large, impressive set. I avoided the purchase with some vague promises.

After that, some friends and their kids who we had invited to join us for dinner phoned to back out. They'd got caught up in all kinds of scheduled activities – as opposed to us, who were just roving around. I was glad, though, because it meant we could go to our favourite restaurant all on our own.

And so we did. The restaurant had wonderful dim lighting and we enjoyed one of the first summer evenings. Although it was almost full, we got a nice table with a two-seater couch. Sitting side by side on the couch, we ordered sodas and our favourite dish, plain spaghetti. I had a glass of wine to celebrate the occasion. We told riddles, teased each other, talked about everything under the sun, and laughed. We were like a contented couple. At some point, the waiter interrupted us because the scooter along with our shopping had slid over to the other side of the restaurant. We burst into fits of giggles and parked it better this time. When the food arrived, my daughter asked me to feed her. In the past I would have grumbled about it. Not anymore. Now I know that these moments are precious, and I let my children lead me down their own magical road.

After paying (she punched the PIN code into the card machine, of course), she figured she could get one last favour out of me. 'Up, Daddy!' she said meaningfully. By that she meant I should hoist her up onto my shoulders and she'd use my head as her steering wheel. Just like we used to. Only now she weighs 30 kilograms, not to mention that the car was almost 300 metres away. I didn't want to refuse her, though, so in one quick movement I swooped her up onto my shoulders. She held onto my ears the way a carriage driver holds the reins of a horse. It was a tad painful, but the pleasure I got from it was far greater. We must have been quite a spectacle: in one hand I had the scooter and in the other the shopping, with my daughter on top. The 300 metres seemed endless. Thank God, though, because the whole way we were cracking up at the prospect of me tripping and us tumbling down onto the pavement, scattering the scooter, the half-bottle of water, the pistachio-green pom-pom, and the unwanted dried fruit every which way. As my daughter laughed, I could feel her tummy jiggling against the nape of my neck. It was 300 metres of sheer joy. When we got to the car, I could hardly feel my neck any more, but I was completely content.

We got in the car and didn't say much. We didn't have to. I drove her to her mother's. As she was getting out, she gave me the tightest hug ever and stayed there, stuck to me, for a few seconds, with her eyes closed. I gave her a kiss and watched her walk away. Just before going through the front door, she turned and shot me one last, joyful look.

It was probably one of the happiest days of my life. You might say we didn't do anything that special, but for me it was everything. It took me a long time, a lot of work, and a lot of pain to learn to live life, to learn the art of living. I now know that moments like these don't come back. I know that the now is the only thing there is.

I know that emotion is my only truth, my only treasure.

I know I adore my children, and all the children of the world, just as they are. They don't need to do anything except be themselves. I know how to enjoy the present. There's no guarantee I'll be alive tomorrow.

It was just one short evening. But for me it was a lifetime.

BE THANKFUL FOR LIFE.

LITTLE BLACK CLOUDS

THEY'RE EVERYWHERE – in cars, on the metro, on the street. They lifelessly plod on as though they're wind-up toys; heads lowered, eyes down, phone in hand. If they're younger, they usually have earphones. They're right out of an episode of *Black Mirror*. On the metro they seem like a funeral procession. And if it happens to be Monday or the weather is bad, or both, they're all even more morose. And don't bump into them by accident or you'll get in trouble. Yes, there are exceptions, but not many.

Unfortunately for them, it's the same in every big city. Eyes glued to their phones, thumbs jabbing away at the screen, almost all ears plugged with headphones. It's a parade of little black clouds. Each one has their own following them everywhere – more loyal than your dog – on the stairs, in the elevator, in the car. Somewhere high up there, the little black clouds unite and become one huge, pitch-black cloud. You could call it emotional smog. And it's toxic – more toxic than anything.

Mobile phones are not entirely to blame, but they add to it. You're having a conversation with a friend and he's got his phone in your face. At the best part of the story, the messages are pinging like crazy. You might be hanging onto your friend's every word, but his mind is on his emails. But you're no different. Even if you're not cradling it, you buzz around it, like a bee around a hive.

You've gone out to dinner with your friend. He gets up to go to the men's room. You can't resist: you reach for your damned phone. And you always have a good excuse: 'I'm expecting an important email, text, call. I have to see what happened.' Bullshit. You're addicted. Like most of us. And it's the most sinister addiction of all. Not only that, it starts early. Our kids are practically born with it.

The more technology advances, offering even more games and apps, the more we withdraw into our hi-tech caves.

The greatest gift you can offer others is your presence.

When you're there, *be* there.

So turn the damned thing off. Leave it at home. It'll change your life. When it's your friend's birthday, call her, don't just post a 'Happy Birthday'. When you wake up in the morning, first hug your partner and then check your messages. When it's just the two of you, look into each other's eyes.

WITHOUT ANY LITTLE BLACK CLOUDS HANGING OVER YOUR HEADS.

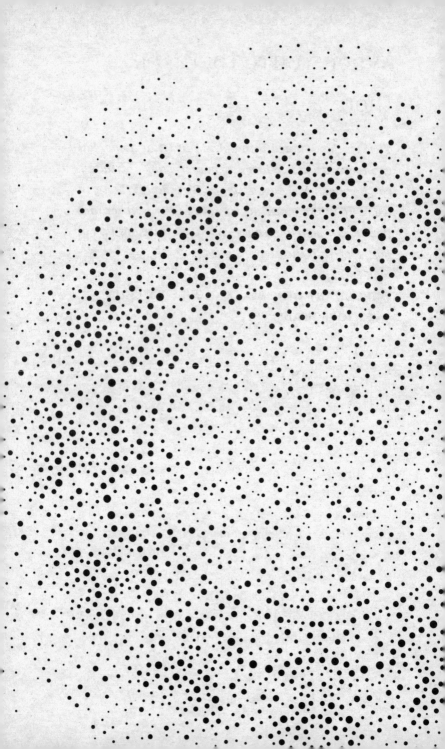

EMMA

ELENI AND I HAD BEEN TRYING TO MEET UP for weeks, if not months, constantly playing phone tag with each other. From the very start, I was thrilled by her vision. A year before, she had experienced the worst thing anyone can go through: she had lost her twenty-four-year-old daughter, Emma, to cancer. Unfortunately, I had never got the chance to meet this beautiful, vivacious, charismatic young woman, full of optimism and lust for life. Her dream had been to create a better life for cancer patients: to have musicians, painters, authors, and other talented people visit them in hospital. They would organise games, movie screenings, and discussions, sharing their talents to help patients become stronger and more optimistic. They would give them a better experience and better odds because a positive mindset means a better immune system.

Eleni and I finally managed to meet up the other day. I had no difficulty picking her out of the crowd.

She was an elegant, dignified woman dressed in black. There was a hint of a smile – as much as the loss of her daughter would allow. She was determined to make Emma's dream come true.

We spoke for a long time. There were sparks in her eyes. Even though the fire of her daughter's existence had burned out, Eleni was able to blow on the last embers and rekindle it. You couldn't tell if the fire belonged to Emma or Eleni for they had now united into one blaze.

'We started in the hospital that embraced our initiative,' she told me.

Special people always say 'we' and 'our'.
Even when they have every reason to say 'I' and 'my'.

'We were given a room to use in the hospital and our idea soon became part of the hospital programme. Everyone there supported us – from the security guards to the last nurse and doctor. Within two weeks, everyone knew about the "Let's do it together" project.'

Special people are always active, even if they have every reason not to be. 'Our vision can't wait,' she told me. 'We've already started, but we need to spread the word and you can help.'

Our meeting lasted about an hour. When we parted, I felt deeply moved and vowed to help Emma's vision come true. I was determined to get to know the unique young woman her daughter was through this wonderful project, even though I would never have the honour of shaking hands with her.

Her name was Emma.

HER NAME IS EMMA.

THE EQUATION

I KNEW AS SOON AS HE WALKED into the store that he was itching to complain. I could tell by his posture: shoulders slumped, hands in pockets, brows knitted, lips drawn back as if to sneeze. He was struggling to hold it in.

'These guys are such a rip-off. I paid 700 euros for the plane ticket and how much do you think they charged to change it? Really, how much?'

'Um, I dunno,' the other guy shrugged.

'Four hundred!' He turned around, hoping for an audience. Our gazes met for a split second, but I quickly looked away. That's all I needed: to get caught in the crossfire.

'And I say, "Dude, I'm changing the ticket a month in advance, not at the last minute. What're you charging me for?"'

And he looked towards the sky, palms upturned in bewilderment, playing the helpless martyr.

I finished what I was doing and rushed out. But I kept thinking about how this guy was wasting his life. Big time. I'm sure he had known about the booking policy before buying the ticket. He just wanted to complain about it. If it wasn't that, it would've been something else.

There are things you can control and things you can't. In school, when we had a maths equation to solve, it was made up of the known and unknown variables. The known ones are a given. The word even says it. What you need to try to do is figure out the unknown variables.

Liars will lie, idiots will say stupid things; in the morning there will be rush-hour traffic, and in the summer it's going to be hot. These are your givens. Now, how you go about dealing with the liar, the stupidities, the traffic, and the heat are your unknown variables. That's your job.

However much you strain against a rooted tree, it won't budge. All you do is waste your energy and put yourself in a bad mood.

We worry about the things we can't control and in the end, we don't have the energy to live our lives.

That's how some people run out of steam and suffer from burnout. They've emptied their gas tank by driving around in circles.

So start by knowing what your given and unknown variables are. That day in the store, the guy with the knitted brows was a given; making a quick getaway was the variable.

I'M STILL MAKING THOSE QUICK GETAWAYS.

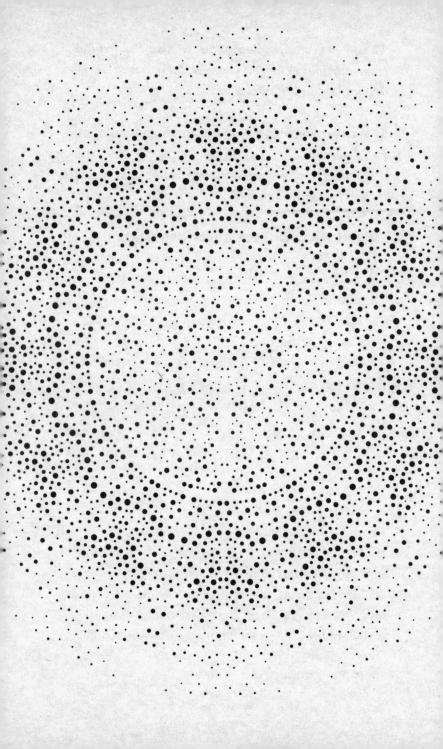

WHY SOME PEOPLE SUCCEED

I T'S WEDNESDAY AFTERNOON AND I'M AT THE CENTRAL FISH MARKET. I walk around, taking in all the smells and listening to the shouts of the fishmongers selling their wares. They soon realise I'm not there to shop and so leave me alone. I pause at one stall without knowing why. They're all the same, I think to myself. But for some reason this one stands out from all the rest. I try to work out how it's different, like we did with those 'spot the difference' quizzes when we were kids.

First difference: the fish are all neatly lined up. Second: the ice is fluffier and whiter, like freshly fallen snow. Third: the stall is so squeaky clean it could be a hospital operating room. Fourth: the people working here keep busy all the time. And they smile. Right when I think I've finished with the quiz, I notice the woman in charge. She's forty-ish, standing in the middle of the space, wearing a spotless, freshly starched apron even though she's probably been there for hours by now. Her rubber boots are shiny clean. She's had her hair done as if for an event. She doesn't shout like the other vendors but, with a paper cone at the ready, she dominates the scene.

Some people have simply chosen success. And success is built on lots of everyday, seemingly insignificant habits. Successful people get to their appointments at least ten minutes early, whether meeting their kid or the US President. They prefer to wait than keep others waiting. Their mobile phone battery never dies on them because they make sure to charge it the night before. If they own a shop, they never run out of change. They stop at red lights because first, they respect themselves and second, they abide by the law. You'll never see them walking along the road wolfing down a sandwich; they will take care of themselves by sitting down at a table for at least five minutes to eat lunch. On the metro, you'll see them reading without bothering anyone and without being bothered. You'll never hear them complaining that they don't have enough time because they make time for everything they do. And they do a lot.

These people live their lives; their lives don't live them. They have learned the art of living. First, they listen and then they speak. They act instead of complaining. They observe instead of judge. When their customers or associates are happy, they're even happier. They truly care about other people. But first of all, they care about themselves and their smiling faces show it. They love what they do. They have what they want because they want what they have. They know how to say no without raising their voice. They see their job as the most important in the world.

These people first have high expectations of themselves, and then of others.

They focus on their goals without getting distracted. They make your day because they've first made sure to make their own day. They don't take themselves too seriously. They know many things, but most of all they know that they don't know everything. These people succeed even when they 'fail'. These people always succeed simply because they've decided to.

JUST LIKE THE WOMAN IN THE IRONED APRON AND THE SHINY RUBBER BOOTS.

HAPPINESS

SOMETIMES IT FEELS LIKE THINGS JUST CLICK, especially when an expert is talking to you.

Something clicked in my head when I watched a charismatic speaker named Dan Gilbert do a TED talk. He was speaking about the science of happiness, giving an example of two men: one has won millions on the lottery; the other becomes a paraplegic in an accident. A year later, the researchers revisit the two men. Who is happier? The lottery winner, right? Wrong. They're equally happy.

The novelty of wealth had grown old very fast for the rich man; he now takes the money he won for granted. Same goes for the disabled man. He's learned to live with his disability. He doesn't like it, but he's grown used to it.

The pursuit of happiness is the reason we are here. Nothing inspiring can happen without it – not your work or your hobby or even your health. Without happiness nothing has meaning.

We sit and wait for happiness to knock on our door. But when the delivery boy arrives with a serving of joy, we don't hear the doorbell because we're lost in our own little worlds.

And yet, happiness is here already. We're the ones who are absent. There is joy to be found when you open your eyes in the morning, in the cold shower that wakes you up, in the last piece of bread in the breadbox, in the car that starts, in the sunshine, and in the warm bed that awaits you at the end of a hard day.

Happiness isn't the actual occurrence of an event. Happiness is the spectacles you wear that enable you to see it, to enjoy it, to allow it to enchant you. If you don't wear the right spectacles, you need to get new ones. They're free of charge.

Happiness is like bread. Learn to bake bread. And when you do, leave the window open.

Leave it open so the whole neighbourhood can smell it, too. And make fresh bread every day.

BREAD GETS STALE FAST.

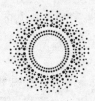

MY ACT OF COURAGE

I VISITED CANADA to attend a presentation by Robin Sharma, one of the world's leading inspirational speakers and author of *The Monk Who Sold His Ferrari*. He is a man who has deeply influenced my life. One of the things I wanted to do in Toronto was visit the landmark CN Tower, the tallest building in the western hemisphere. I had read that you could do the EdgeWalk, a hands-free stroll along the 1168-foot-high ledge that circles around the top of the Tower's main pod, while attached to a rail by a harness.

Growing up, I remember being scared all the time – scared to raise my hand in class, scared to say 'no' to someone, scared to do what I wanted and stand up for myself. I never acted up or got rowdy, of course. Plus, I had a fear of heights.

I visited the Tower without having decided whether I'd go for the EdgeWalk. I told myself I'd decide on the spot. I went over to the booking counter and the young lady suggested I watch the video to help me make up my mind. That didn't help either. The spectacle was truly frightening. I watched it again and again but still couldn't make a decision. Fear had become part of my life and so had the pain that goes with it.

But I was sick of this fear and sick of myself. And suddenly, I made the decision to go for it. I was taken to a room to be fitted with the special uniform and harness.

When three of us emerged on the one-hundred-and-twentieth floor, the guide told me to go out onto the ledge first. It was windy as hell out there and I was terrified. Then I gradually started easing into it and feeling a little more comfortable. We were out on the ledge for half an hour, and I ended up enjoying it. I didn't expect to, but I did.

I have owed myself this little act of courage for years. It was like unlocking the prison cell that I had gone to great pains to create for myself and I had finally escaped for good.

In this deal with myself I didn't back down. I didn't slink away.

Fortunately, after so many years I have learned not to shrink back in fear, but to step forward, even if there are gale-force winds out there. The lesson had finally sunk in.

Your act of courage might be finally going to the gym you've signed up for or making that phone call to a beloved friend or maybe finishing that project that's been collecting dust in the drawer. Maybe it's taking steps to live the life you're not currently living. I don't know what it means for you, but it's none of my business after all.

Only you know what it is.

Only you can do it.

TODAY. NOT TOMORROW.

I LOVE YOU

I HAVE A FRIEND NAMED ELIAS and he's a rare breed. He's a real fighter and doesn't think twice about starting over if he has to. To him, no obstacle is too great. He's the strong, silent type. Just looking at him makes you feel proud.

We meet up two or three times a year and share everything about our lives with each other on those few occasions. We hug, laugh heartily, and enjoy one another. We delight in each other's happiness and console each other in sad times.

I tried calling him on his birthday. We were finally able to speak the third time I called, and he was overjoyed to hear from me. Sometimes emotions can be so strong that you can feel them over the phone – the smiles, the gestures, the excitement. That's how it was when we spoke. The call didn't last more than five minutes, and even though we hadn't spoken for six months, we said and felt everything that was needed. We arranged to meet a couple of weeks later. But he saved the best for last: 'Hey, Stefanos, I love you, man . . .'

I was stunned. I didn't know how to react. I got all choked up. I don't remember what or even *if* I answered. It was like a tsunami of joy had washed over me.

We usually don't tell people how we feel. But it's what we live for; it's what makes us human. The last thing people trapped in the Twin Towers on 9/11 did was call their loved ones to tell them how much they loved them. Those were their final words.

We tend to save these words for the end. We're stingy with them or afraid of them and so often don't say them when we should. Especially us men. We're afraid of being vulnerable or affectionate, but that's what life is all about.

A man who lost his son in a car accident said it all in his eulogy: 'We make the mistake of believing there will always be a tomorrow. But sometimes that tomorrow never comes. And then we regret all we didn't say or do. The last time I told you I loved you, son, was when you called me to wish me happy birthday. And I still remember – and always will – how happy I was when you answered, "I love you, too, Dad." I never said it again after that.'

So go say your 'I love you's today, my friend. Say it to the person you need to and don't overthink it.

Life is just one breath.
Sometimes tomorrow
never comes.

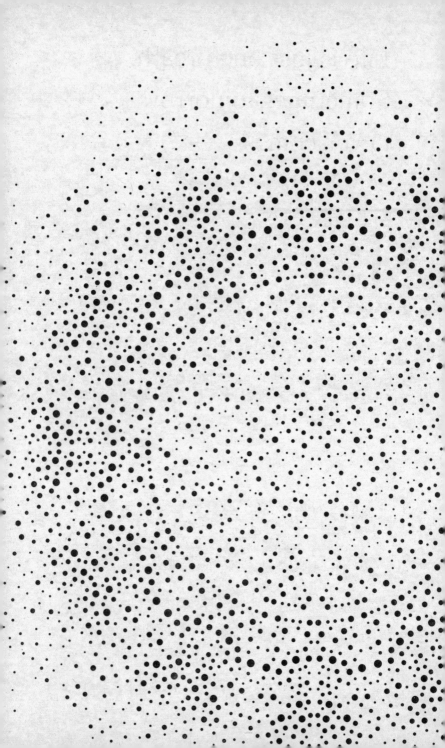

TERRIFIC!

I USED TO SAY IT ALL THE TIME when I wanted to describe something I liked. It was mostly out of habit and because I had heard other people say it: 'Terrific!'

When I first went to my mentor Antonis's workshop, I noticed that no one used words like 'terrific' or 'incredible'. It was as if there was a ban on those words. But they would say things like 'excellent', 'superb', and 'amazing'. But I kept singing the same old tune: 'terrific this', 'terrific that'.

At some point, a friend pulled me aside and told me the secret. 'We don't use words like that here,' he informed me discreetly enough not to offend me, but firmly enough that I wouldn't forget.

'Why not?'

'The word terrific comes from "terror". "Incredible" means you are not able to believe it. We avoid using negative words to describe something positive,' he explained. 'If you're sowing a handful of seeds, would you want them to be infested with parasites?'

'No.' I got the message. Words shape your life. So use them wisely. Words and life are like the chicken or the egg question: your life creates the words you use, and the words you use create your life.

Your whole life can alter if you change just one word in your vocabulary.

When somebody asks you how it's going, don't say, 'My life's so hectic.'

SAY SOMETHING POSITIVE.

SIGALAS AND OSEOLA

I HANG ON HIS EVERY WORD. He has a unique sense of wisdom and calm about him and I want to soak it all up. Mohammed is from Alexandria, Egypt, and he's my eighty-year-old coach in squash and life.

I love it when he tells me stories about Alexandria in the 1950s. He played basketball at university and has a true sense of sportsmanship, which he's passed on to me and the others he tirelessly coaches. Mohammed told me about the sponsors supporting the Greek team he used to play with in Alexandria. The players had heard about but never seen their team sponsor, a Mr Sigalas. They assumed he was some rich Greek tycoon. One day, he appeared at practice as the players were leaving the court. He seemed a humble, unassuming man. One of the boys asked his coach what Mr Sigalas did for a living. 'He's a mail clerk,' the coach replied.

Sigalas had scrimped and saved to help out the boys on the basketball team.

Wealth isn't having. Wealth is giving.

Sharing is amazing. And it's the only way to be happy. Share something everywhere you go: a flower, a book, a hug, a good word, a wish. Leave the world a better place than you found it.

You've been put on this earth to share, to help, and to love. On your deathbed you won't think back to how much money you made, but to how much love you gave and got. That's the only thing that counts.

There was a woman from Mississippi called Oseola MacCarty. No one really knew of her, but now she's world famous and was awarded the Presidential Citizens Medal by Bill Clinton. An African-American washerwoman, Oseola had no children and worked her fingers to the bone, putting her hard-earned money away in a bank account. One day, she went to the bank and the teller said, 'Do you know how much money you've saved, Oseola?'

'How much?'

'250,000 dollars! You're rich,' he told her. Oseola couldn't grasp how much that was. To help her understand, the teller put ten dimes on the counter. 'Let's say this is the money you've saved. How would you like to distribute it?'

She thought for a moment and said, 'One dime for the church, one for each of my three nephews, and let me think about the other six.' A few days later, Oseola hobbled into the University of South Mississippi to meet the Dean. She handed him a check for 150,000 dollars.

'It's for the black kids,' she said, 'the ones who want to go to college, but don't have the money.' And she smiled at him.

THAT'S WHAT YOU'RE HERE FOR.

RECIPE FOR SPAGHETTI

FIRST YOU NEED WATER. Water is everything. Up to 60 per cent of our body is water. It pumps the heart, cleanses our bodies, assists with weight loss, and makes your skin glow. They also call it brain fuel. I was amazed to read that drinking water can increase the efficiency of the brain by up to 30 per cent. Since I learned that fact, I've made a point of drinking a lot of water. And as far as cooking spaghetti goes, not enough water means the spaghetti sticks to the pan, and none at all means a burnt pot.

Then you need some salt. Without salt your spaghetti will be tasteless. The salt of life is called dopamine and it is the basic ingredient of happiness. It gives people a sense of joy and euphoria, providing physical and mental wellbeing. Where do you find it? In every good deed you do, even the ones you think might be trivial, like picking up a piece of litter, opening the door for a stranger, buying a friend a drink, surprising your family, or helping those in need. When you share or do the right thing, your body secretes dopamine, and lots of it. So don't poo-poo the do-gooders. They're the smart ones. Looking out for number one is easy, but it will cost you more than you think. It'll cost you your happiness.

And don't forget about adding some butter to your pasta dish, too. Your life needs a little butter. It's called endorphins and you can find them in sports and exercise. They boost the neuroplasticity of the brain and its ability to learn and retain information and make decisions. Endorphins have been called a natural anti-depressant, a natural high.

If you're wanting to serve meatballs with your spaghetti, then don't forget to take the mince out of the freezer well in advance.

Plan ahead, like any good cook does when making a dish.

But it seems we've forgotten a basic ingredient: the spaghetti! In life it's called action and it's the main ingredient. I hear people talking, judging, and complaining, but I see few who actually act. I see many who sell off their dream for peanuts. It's true that the couch is comfy, but getting too comfortable kills you and your dream. Action is waking up early and organising your day. Action is giving your all at work even if you're underpaid. Action is doing something instead of complaining about it. So shut up and act.

It all depends on you. If you've been told the cook has no control over the recipe, then you've been fooled.

There was a farmer out in his garden getting some sun. His wife went over and asked him what he was doing.

'I'm waiting for my crops to grow,' he tells her.

'But you haven't even ploughed the field or sowed the seeds,' she replied.

'Never mind,' he says. 'They'll grow.'

MOST OF US ARE LIKE THE FARMER. WE THINK THINGS WILL HAPPEN BY THEMSELVES.

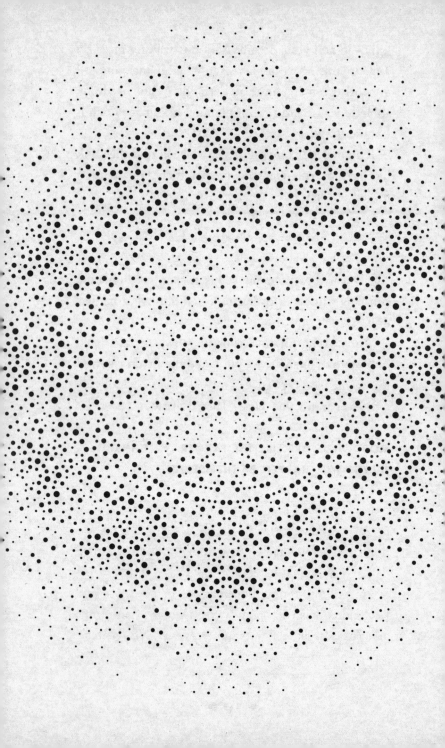

WHATEVER . . .

I WAS STANDING IN ONE OF TWO CASHIER LINES. A cheerful, young man was at the front of the other line. He and the cashier were having a spirited conversation.

At some point, I must have missed one or two of their exchanges, because when the cashier next told him something, I heard him mutter disappointedly in reply, 'Whatever . . .' It was as if he had suddenly changed into a different person. His voice was flat and lifeless. Even his posture had changed: shoulders slumped forward, head lowered, hands stuffed in his pockets. All of a sudden, he had transformed into a sorry-looking soul.

I was upset. I recognised in him what so many of us do to ourselves, though we don't mean to. We don't realise what we are doing and how much damage it can cause.

I'm talking about the illness of helplessness and I wouldn't wish it on my worst enemy. Symptoms are phrases like 'What can I say?', 'Who cares?'

'Whatever', 'It's no big deal', 'Who gives a f**k?' And these symptoms will sap your energy, your optimism, your spirit, and your dreams. They suck the very life out of you.

A few, apparently small, lapses in control on a daily basis can lead to disaster in the long run. You smoke a cigarette. (One little ciggie isn't going to kill me, right?) You eat junk food. (There's no harm in a bag of nachos, is there?) You curl up in front of the TV. (I deserve to relax, don't I?) Diet? (I'll start on Monday.) Reading? (I'm too busy right now.) Have that talk with my kid? (I'll do it tomorrow.) My dream project? (Let's get through this recession first.)

There are all kinds of illnesses out there. One thing is for sure, though. If you don't look after yourself, you're going to get sick.

I'll never know what that cashier said to make the young man wither. But I can tell you this: a 'whatever' a day keeps your life away.

I once read this and I thought it was brilliant:

The definition of Hell:
on your last day on Earth

you meet the person you could have been.

SO STEER CLEAR OF THOSE 'WHATEVERS'.

HOME SWEET HOME

HE WAS SWIMMING LAZILY a little further down the beach. It was all too clear he was enjoying himself, like he had hung a 'Do Not Disturb' sign on the door. I decided to try, nonetheless, to strike up a conversation with him. 'Good morning,' I said.

'Good morning!' he replied abruptly, as if he'd been woken from a trance. But then he went on to tell me his story. 'I'm Greek as well, but I live in Russia. I had to go abroad to work to provide for my family. We come here every year for a month on vacation. I swim here every morning, afternoon, and evening. We've been here twenty days and have another ten to go. I count them one by one. We have a sea there, too – the Black Sea. No comparison. It's paradise here. The sun, the crystal-clear water, the warm weather . . .' And then he said something I'll never forget: 'Ahh, Greece! Home sweet home!' His eyes teared up. And so did mine.

How many things we take for granted . . . our home, our family, our friends, our health. And then, as soon as some stumbling block crops up, as it inevitably will, we think back to the past when we were healthier and happier, but we didn't know it. And so we're happy for a bit until we forget about it again.

Why aren't we more thankful for what we have in the present?

It's called gratitude and it's probably the most powerful way you can transform your life.

There once was a poor farmer, who lived with his wife and six children in a house that was too small for them. One day he visits the village wise man.

'O, Wise Man, there's not enough room in our home.'

The wise man thinks for a bit.

'Do you have a dog?' he asks the family man.

'I do.'

'Keep him in the house.'

'But, Wise Man, we can hardly fit ourselves.'

'Do as I say and come back next week.'

The following week the family man returns to the wise man. 'How did it go?'

'It's even worse now. The dog kept us up all night.'

'Do you have a goat?'

'I do.'

'Keep the goat in the house, too.'

'But, Wise Man . . .'

'Do as I say.'

The following week the man goes back. 'How did it go?'

'Terribly! Now the dog fights with the goat.'

'Do you have a cow?'

'I do.'

'Keep it in the house.'

'But . . .'

'Do as I say.'

The following week he goes back. 'How did it go?'

'Things couldn't be worse. All the animals fight, the cow moos like crazy, the children can't sleep . . .'

'Now this is what you're going to do: put all the animals back in the barnyard, so it's just the eight of you.'

The man goes back a week later. 'How did it go?'

'Perfect! Things couldn't be better!' the family man says enthusiastically.

'Good,' says the wise man.

'AREN'T YOU HAPPY WITH THE ROOM YOU HAVE NOW?'

CATCH THE BALL

SHE SOUNDED UPSET on the phone. I was worried at first because she usually speaks calmly. This time, even her breathing was uneven. She blurted out the whole story.

'I had this nagging feeling that I should call her [her best friend]. She sounded terrible on the phone. Worse than ever. "What's wrong, sweetie?" I asked her.'

'I'm in a bad way.'

'I'm coming over.'

'No, don't. I won't be good company.'

My friend immediately rushed over to see her friend, who had been out of work for a long time and whose finances were a mess. She and her husband couldn't support their family anymore. She had reached rock bottom.

At the very moment she was consoling her friend, her mobile rang.

'I considered letting it ring, Stefanos,' she told me, 'because it was such bad timing. But something inside me told me to pick up. It was my friend Vasilis, who'd just got a great job at Company X, who operate in exactly the line of work my miserable best friend was in. She's brilliant at what she does, by the way. And guess what? Company X was hiring! And guess who had just been put in charge of Human Resources? My friend, Vasilis! Plus, he owes me a favour. Pure chance, or what?'

They were able to arrange an interview for her on the spot. Everything happens for a reason. We call it luck or coincidence, but it's not. There's a reason for everything and a time for everything. Call it a plan if you will. An argument, a phone call, or a conversation happens at a particular time so that it can tell you something. They're like the perfect passes the players on the Dream Team make. Sometimes you'll get passes like those. So make sure you catch the ball. And don't hold onto it for too long. Throw a pass like my friend did. Pick up that phone, make that appointment, and go see that person.

Somewhere inside there's a little voice that always knows what to do. Learn to listen to it.

There was a very religious man shipwrecked on a desert island. One day a ship passes by.

'Shall we save you?'

'No, God will save me.'

A while later, another ship passes by. 'Shall we save you, my man?'

'No, God will save me,' he replied again.

One day a helicopter passes overhead. It lands and the pilot gets out. 'Shall I save you?' he asks.

'No, God will save me. He won't forget me.'

After a while, our friend arrives at the pearly gates.

'Why, dear God, did you forget me? I was waiting for you to save me,' he complains.

'I SENT YOU *THREE* SAVIOURS, SILLY MAN!'

SPARKLING WATER

I'VE BEEN OBSESSED WITH SPARKLING MINERAL WATER for years. My daughters call it 'bubbles'. It quenches our thirst and we feel really refreshed when we drink it. We drink cases of it.

There's one bad thing about it, though: it often runs out in stores. Whenever I find it at the supermarket, I make sure to stock up. Fortunately, I've found a small grocery shop that always seems to have some.

I stop by there to return the used bottles and order three more boxes: thirty-six bottles in total. We arrange a time for the delivery, and they are always punctual.

When the doorbell rings at 4 p.m., I'm sure it's the delivery boy. I can hear him outside the building lugging the boxes – this is thirty-six litres we're talking about! I go down to the entrance and open the door. He's a young guy wearing sunglasses, in his mid-thirties, balding with a stubbly beard – a fashionable combo in recent years. He's sweaty, tired, and irritated; the type of guy you don't want to mess with. He's curt.

'Is there an elevator?' He doesn't want to hear the word 'no'.

'Yes, there is. Third floor.'

He hauls the boxes up. 'Where do you want 'em?'

I show him. He's now completely exhausted and out of breath.

I had informed the store I'd be paying by card. I have it ready, plus a two-euro tip. I was going to give him two and a half, but his gruff manner told me not to.

'I'll have to come back,' he says, trying to hide his frustration.

'Why?' (I know very well why.)

'I forgot to bring the POS machine.' His voice is a mere gasp at this point.

He turns to leave, head down. Something tells me to stop him. 'I can pay you in cash,' I say.

'Would you do that?' He's surprised.

'Of course I would.'

We're both happy. He hands me the receipt for €35.40. I give him a €50 bill. He prepares to give me €14.60 in change. I take the €10 bill out of his hand. 'Keep the change.'

He can't believe it. Too good to be true. And then his face lights up and he grins from ear to ear as if he's just won the lottery when he was down to his last coppers.

'Thank you,' he says. 'Thank you.'

'Can I get you a glass of water, man?'

'No. No, thanks.'

'Thank you,' I say.

'No, thank *you*.'

He gets in the elevator and gives me the kindest look I can remember: head slightly bowed, eyelids lowered slowly, and his right hand softly touches his heart. He's smiling from head to toe.

The elevator door closes, but the look remains with me.

I just made someone's day. I shut the front door. I am alone and my eyes have welled up with gratitude. I just might be the happiest man on Earth right now.

Thank you.

THANK YOU.

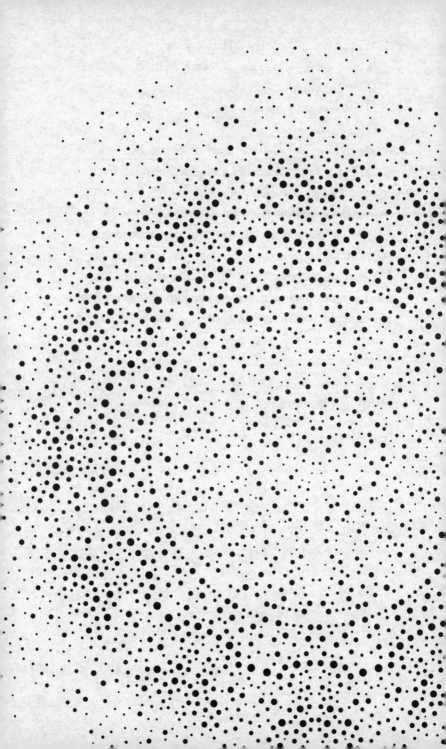

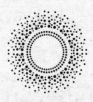

CLOSE THE WINDOWS

SHE'S MY HOMEOPATH. On occasion, my psychoanalyst and sometimes my teacher, too. Every time I meet her, I come away a wiser man.

This incident happened a while ago. I was stressed and suffering with various symptoms. There were a hundred different things going on inside my head. She looked at me with an understanding smile, as always.

Turning her laptop towards me, she started opening windows on the screen – never-ending windows. At first, I didn't catch on to what she was doing. At some point, the screen froze. We both sat there and stared at it.

'What makes you think your brain is any different?' she asked me. 'We open window after window and, at some point, the poor thing crashes. We think we can do everything, that we're superhuman. We're wrong.' I'll never forget those words.

We live in a time of multi-tasking. When you try to do everything at once, in the end very little gets done. You do a half-arsed job of everything, as they say.

At times, I feel that as fast as technology is advancing, we are reversing. We're here, but we're not present.

The best gift you can give those around you is your presence.

When you're there, really be there. Don't spread yourself around. Better to spend one hour with someone and really be present than ten minutes and be distracted the whole time. And this goes for everyone and everything: your child, your partner, your friend, your work, your writing, your book, your thoughts – anything you choose to do. There's nothing else in that moment, nothing else exists. Live just for that and devote your whole being to it. Focus. Only then are you there, only then do you honour what you're doing, only then do you honour life. And yourself.

The Greeks have a saying for it: you can't fit two watermelons under one arm.

Nowadays, they might call it single-tasking. Sometimes I think that we just rediscover wise, old adages and reword them to make them sound cool.

MR IOANNIDIS

I WORSHIPPED HIM. I have this thing for the elderly: respect for the wisdom of these silent heroes in our lives. They deserve to be honoured for all they've given.

Mr Ioannidis – that's what I always called him – was my colleague when I worked at Sky TV. He taught me the job and taught me about life. It was as if he sucked out life's very marrow. He was a dynamic cosmopolitan, a man of class. He was also a man of emotion and wasn't afraid to show it, always smiling and leaving his mark wherever he went, along with the scent of his cologne.

He always handled the big clients. To be precise, he took on small clients and turned them into big ones in his own special way. Among his many tools were persuasion and sincerity, logic and sound arguments, empathy and feeling, trust and appreciation. He was one of a kind and the clients loved him.

He had a real passion for music. He had tens of thousands of tracks in his digital collection and was more adept than a fifteen-year-old at using the software. He loved creating his own playlists and then giving them away as presents, with songs ranging from Aznavour to Zappa.

He never stopped working, even when he retired. Every month he'd stop by my office for a chat and when he did, everyone would poke their heads in to say hello to him, hoping, perhaps, that some of his lust for life would rub off on them.

A few years ago, his beloved wife, Nana, called me. Her voice trembled when I answered. 'Stefanos, Nikos passed away . . .' She burst into tears and so did I.

We said our last goodbyes at a suburban cemetery one sunny winter afternoon. How do you part with a person who was so full of life? Here's how: not with tears but with smiles. As we sipped our coffee at the coffeehouse following the funeral service, we all overflowed with reminiscences about times we'd spent with Nikos Ioannidis. And we laughed with our hearts – and without a shred of decorum. Even his wife joined in. We celebrated his life; perhaps that was the most beautiful day I'd spent with him.

I promised Nana I would keep in touch on a regular basis and that made her very happy. But I never did.

The other day, Mr Ioannidis's son, Yorgos, called me.

'How are you, Yorgos? How are your kids? So nice to hear from you!'

'We're fine, Stefanos. But I don't have good news. Mother passed away yesterday. I went over to her house and found she had passed away in her sleep.' I just sat there holding the phone. 'Stefanos, are you there?'

'She went to join your father, Yorgos,' I managed to say.

'Yes, Stefanos. That's exactly it. The funeral's tomorrow at 3 p.m. The same place where we buried Dad.'

I will never see Nana again. So, don't put things off, my friend.

Sometimes that damned tomorrow never dawns.

TAKE CARE OF YOURSELF

I T'S SUNDAY NIGHT. I've done my run, written in my journal, and I decide to go and see a good movie at the open-air cinema.

Not much time to shower after my run, though. I'll probably just change into dry clothes, I think. But this doesn't sit well with me, so I reconsider. I make the snap decision to jump into the shower. I wash off the sweat, dry myself properly, and look at myself in the mirror. I look presentable.

Clothes now. On the hanger are my Bermuda shorts and the T-shirt I was wearing this morning, a little wrinkled but clean. I go to put them on but change my mind. Though I'm cutting it really fine, I open the drawer and take out a pair of freshly ironed Bermudas. I feel good. I pick a crisp, new shirt from the wardrobe. Both are nice, and they look even better together.

Now for shoes. My running shoes are next to the door. I'm not happy with these either. I wear my street shoes. I check myself in the mirror again.

Everything looks good. But it's one of the last summer nights of September. What if it's a little chilly out? I take a sweatshirt with me just in case. I stuff a twenty-euro bill in my back pocket and I'm all set.

But I change my mind about this, too. I switch it to a fifty-euro bill. What if I want to go all out tonight? Shouldn't I have enough money? I hop into my car and set off. I catch a glimpse of myself in the mirror. I'm looking good.

I get to the open-air cinema five minutes before the movie starts. I treat myself to a drink, find a good seat to sit and enjoy the trailers. I couldn't be happier.

Taking care of yourself is key.
It makes you feel good, important even.
It makes you feel you deserve all this.

When you're looking after yourself, the most important person in your life – you – is honouring you. And you can't put a price on that.

We often give ourselves the leftovers of life. I used to do that all the time. My old self never complained, never said a word, but I know how good my self feels when I look after him, when I show him how much I appreciate and love him. He soars.

The movie is excellent. I go to the restroom during the intermission. There is a respectable, middle-aged man there, too. I get out of the stall first and go to the sink on the right. Then the man comes out and I move to the other sink to make things easier for him. I smile at him and he returns the smile and thanks me.

'Good movie,' I say.

'Very,' he replies.

'Take care,' I tell him on his way out.

'You, too,' he says.

YES, TAKE CARE.

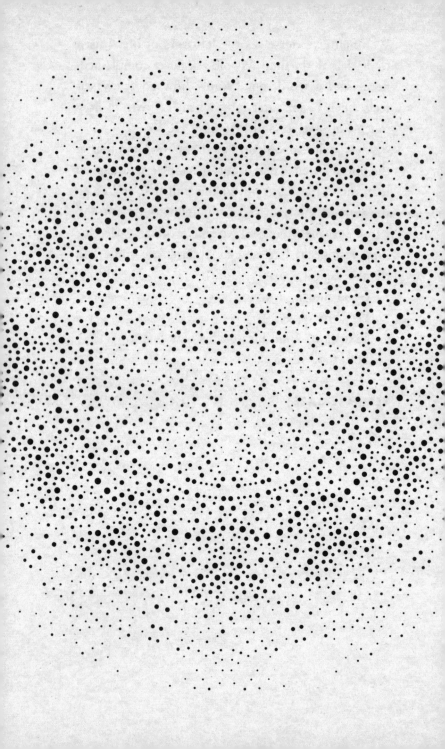

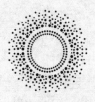

BULLYING

SOME PARENTS DRIVE ME CRAZY. These people have always got on my nerves, but ever since I had kids, they've started to really piss me off.

Some parents choose to live through their kids. Though they manipulate their offspring in the worst way, they consider themselves, and others like them, to be excellent parents. They don't respect their children, because they essentially don't respect themselves. They fill them with fear because they don't have the guts to face their own fears. Instead of re-examining their own lives, they chauffeur their kids to ballet classes, swimming pools, karate lessons, and sports fields all day long. In fact, they are the ones who decide which activity their kids will do and get angry when their children disagree. They even pick out the clothes they wear, the subjects they should like best, the emotions they should feel, the relationships they should cultivate, the career they will follow, and, ultimately, the life they will live – if the poor things can call that a life, that is.

They choose their children's friends based on the

parents they themselves are compatible with. They choose which foods their kids eat, which party they will go to; they even decide at which temperature they should feel cold. When their kids desperately try to communicate their deepest feelings, these parents pay them little or no attention. Instead, they take advantage of their wider vocabulary to shut them up.

And when these kids grow up and turn forty, their parents continue to badger them as if they were still four-year-olds. With few exceptions, these 'kids' won't manage to stand on their own two feet even in their fifties. If and when they finally realise how toxic their parents are, they will be filled with resentment and their parents will wonder why. Why? Because they have to be given the opportunity to live their own lives.

But I really blow my top when one of these parents – yes, the ones who ruin their children 24/7 – panics because another child supposedly bullied their precious darling. When another kid kicks theirs during break time, this parent becomes furious and starts blaming the teachers, the school, other parents, the authorities. It is impossible for this person to accept that the most destructive bullying is their own behaviour towards their child.

I heard an outstanding educator suggest that we should treat our children as equal to us in one of his talks. But it takes guts to turn your back on what you think is the easiest solution: that is, dominating – or even worse, living through – your children.

Children need parents who will show them the roads but not lead them down them.

Or, at least, who won't pressure them to take the most 'preferable' route.

Children need parents who will support their own decisions, even when they don't agree with them. The poet Kahlil Gibran wisely wrote:

> Your children are not your children . . .
> They come through you but not from you.
> And though they are with you yet they belong
>   not to you.
> You may give them your love but not your
>   thoughts,
> For they have their own thoughts.*

---

* From *The Prophet*, Knopf, 1923

In the famous scene from the movie *Philadelphia*, just before the trial, Tom Hanks's character, Andrew Beckett, prepares his parents for the difficult moments that will follow in court:

'I can't imagine there is anything that anyone could say that would make us feel less proud of you,' his father tells him.

'I don't expect any of my kids to sit in the back of the bus,' his mother says proudly.

'I love you guys,' Andrew responds tearfully.

THOSE ARE THE KIND OF PARENTS WE WANT.

LEAVE A DOOR OPEN

I WAS IN THE MIDDLE OF WRITING THIS BOOK when my mobile phone pinged. It was a video message from my daughter. She was with her mother, babysitting her little cousin, and she had sent me the lyrics to a song I used to sing to her before she went to sleep when she was a baby. She would stare at me wide-eyed while I sang. After a while, her little eyes would close while she held my hand tightly on her belly. It will always be our song, until the very end . . .

Now she's nine and she's rediscovered the song. I don't see her or her little sister every day anymore. But they will always live deep inside me in a special place. However much they grow up, however much I grow old, wherever they go and wherever I go . . .

I read the lyrics and remember those magical moments when I would sing to her, and I feel something stir within me, something very strong. My eyes tear up and I can feel what my little girl felt when she read them. *My daddy used to sing this to me and now I'm going send it back to him.* I can feel how excited she was for me to read it. For a moment I become her.

I give in to the feeling and let it wash over me. I savour it. I become the emotion and let it course through my body, no holds barred, no signposts to tell it where to go, no speed limit. I know that I'll never feel this exact emotion again.

It hasn't always been this way. I used to hide my feelings. I was embarrassed.

We men have been cursed from birth. We're told that men don't cry. That men are strong. Give me a break.

Luckily, I now know that vulnerability makes you strong.

Vulnerability is someone who cries, buckles under pressure, and who sometimes can't handle it.

Back in the day, my grandma would never lock the door to her house and sometimes even leave it open.

Friends blew in, the wind blew in, and life blew in.

And that's how I've decided to live my life: with the door open, so the sun can come in.

To wake me up.

To keep me warm.

BE WELL, MY SWEET LITTLE GIRL.

THE THIEF

SOME PEOPLE ARE AFRAID OF THIEVES. They're afraid they'll steal their money, rob their house, or take their children.

But there's another kind of thief that's sneakier and a lot more dangerous: the one within us. This one's a pro. He steals from us every day and without making a sound. This thief robs us of our dreams, optimism, joy, inspiration, discipline, and energy. He steals our very life.

But we've become one with this thief and don't realise he's even there. He's like those termites hidden inside wooden beams, slowly but surely eating away at us.

There's a story I heard from India. An old man was talking to his grandson. 'You have two wolves inside you,' he tells the boy. 'One is bad. It is anger, envy, sadness, disappointment, greed, sarcasm, self-pity, offensiveness, inferiority, vanity, arrogance, and egotism. The other wolf is good. It is joy, love, hope, peace, serenity, humility, kindness, charity, empathy, generosity, and faith in God.'

The boy, who was listening attentively, finally asked his grandfather, 'And who will win?'

The old man thought for a moment and then replied, 'The one you feed the most.'

Every wolf has its favourite foods. The bad wolf likes lots of TV, wasting time on social media, sticking his nose into other people's business, criticising others, gossiping, whining, lying, eating junk, staying up too late, playing it safe, lazing around, toxic people, routine, resentment, prejudice, and indifference. The good wolf feeds on love, truth, kindness, gratitude, self-respect, focus, action, constant development, responsibility, organisation, exercising, drinking lots of water, standing up straight, waking up early, and working hard.

Feeding the bad wolf and expecting it not to grow is like eating cake and hoping you'll lose weight.

Always keep the good wolf well fed. It keeps the thieves away.

THAT'S YOUR JOB.

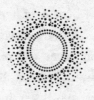

THE LIFEGUARD

SLIM, ELEGANT, AND SPORTING A WIDE HEADBAND. You couldn't help but notice her. But her self-assurance almost seemed to border on conceit.

It was our last day at the hotel and we should have already left if we were hoping to check-out on time. But since I'm not very good at putting my foot down with my daughters – something they know too well – my eldest was able to squeeze in a couple of final goes on the waterslide.

This pretty lifeguard was on duty. She spent most of her time chatting with a co-worker. While my daughter was going down the slide, the girl was constantly adjusting her headband, gathering up her hair, tucking in the lose strands, making a big production of it all. Her vanity appeared boundless, as if she was God's gift to the world. For some reason, the more she preened, the more irritated I got.

My eldest was taking her last go down the slide, and her little sister was craning her neck to try to watch her but she couldn't get a good view. Somehow, the lifeguard realised what my little one wanted. In one swift move, she bent over, tenderly lifted her up and safely set her on the ledge so she could see. I was startled for a moment and so was my youngest, but she didn't show it because she was so focused on her sister. After my eldest had gone down the slide, my little one beamed a grateful smile at the lifeguard, who gave her a tender hug and slowly brought her down from the ledge. My daughter just stared at her, happy and impressed.

The pretty lifeguard turned towards me and smiled discreetly. I returned the smile. The fatigue from the long day vanished at once. I stood to the side of the pool and laughed to myself. Then, I collected the girls and we left.

I remembered a great saying that I had read recently:

Don't judge me just because I sin differently from you.

THE DRUMMER

I'VE SEEN HIM BEFORE. He's always dressed in black with sunglasses perched on a head of fairly conventional hair for a drummer. But I've never seen him like this before. Today he stole my heart and mind. For the three minutes that he performed his solo, I existed on another plane – I don't know where it was, but it was certainly alongside him.

It was a school performance and we parents had been invited along to enjoy the musicians. He stepped onto the stage as silently as a cat. He started playing and the drums gradually began to get louder and more intense. In those three magical minutes, the guy was staring off somewhere into the distance – I don't know where, but he was in some kind of bliss. Part of him was there and part was with us. He had split himself in two and then became one again – an extraordinary One.

The finale was approaching and the climax with it. When it was over, we applauded loudly. But the guy wasn't listening. He just kept staring into his bliss as if something inside him was saying, 'I'm ready. Come take me whenever you want.'

Some people don't know how to live otherwise. All of their emotions are heightened; they are happy to experience both joy and pain, because they know you have to experience pain in life. People like this know that they will get knocked down, and are prepared to get back up again. They know how to give everything they've got, even when they have little left to give.

They can't stand a middle-of-the-road kind of life. They're not afraid of losing anything because everything they need is already within them. They didn't come here to have a good time, but to give it their all. They are prepared to die fighting for their passions. They give everything when they are playing on stage, peering through the microscope, or writing their manuscript. Their passion is their life.

A life without passion is not worth living.

FIND YOUR PASSION IN LIFE.

TALK TO YOURSELF

WHEN I WAS A KID, I HATED ARTICHOKES. Now, they're my favourite food. So I've decided that I should let a few more new things into my life – who knows where my next new favourite thing will turn up?

If someone had told me years ago to talk to myself, I would have laughed in their face. But as it turns out, you really need to try it! I first read about affirmations in a book by Louise Hay. An affirmation is everything you tell yourself, whether or not you say it out loud, whether or not you even realise you're doing it. Every day, the brain has 40,000 thoughts, one every two seconds. Most thoughts are subconscious, and they are usually negative. A child of ten has already been subjected to thousands of hours of lecturing from home, school, or via the media. All those 'no's and 'don't's are seeds that take root, then sprout, and finally they produce fruit – one every two seconds.

Most parents are supportive until their children take their first step and say their first word. Then, the majority unknowingly hold their children back, just like their own parents did to them. 'Watch out!', 'You're going to fall!', 'That's not for you', and so on. They sow the worst seed in their offspring: the seed of helplessness. And most children believe it. They believe they can't determine their own lives, and that they're worthless. And they end up not liking themselves and battling with life.

The mind now needs new seedlings because it's overgrown with weeds.

Affirmations are the new seeds that you, yourself, plant in your brain.

Your affirmations are your new truth.

So you sit in front of the mirror and you tell yourself good things. Many times. Over and over again. Until you believe it. It might takes months or even years. It took years to fill your brain with negativity, and so replacing it with positivity will take time. Make your affirmations early in the morning, as soon as you wake up, and again at night before you go to bed, when the soil for sowing them is nice and light. Say them in the present tense, and phrase them in a positive way. And they should only be about you because you do not determine anyone else's mind.

The girls and I have been making affirmations for years now. 'I am worth it' is one of them and we say it a hundred times every morning and night. The more you say it, the more you believe it. And the more you believe it, the better you feel. Your affirmation is your seed. Of course, you need to water it, tend to it, and fertilise it for it to grow. That is what we call *action*.

One day my six-year-old daughter tells me, 'Hey, Dad. You know what happens when I say, "I am worth it" over and over?'

'What?'

'I smile. Without meaning to.'

That's what affirmations do. They make your soul smile.

WITHOUT MEANING TO . . .

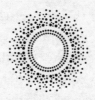

HOW TO SUCCEED

MIDDAY ON A CENTRAL ROAD in Athens: as I'm walking along, a small, three-wheeler truck stops at the side of the road next to a recycling bin without blocking the traffic, parking lights flashing. Out gets a well-groomed man, neatly dressed in black trousers and shirt, and shined shoes. He heads for the bin.

Intrigued, I stop to watch him. He carefully opens the lid of the bin and scans the contents. He chooses only the cardboard boxes and, taking a box cutter from his pocket, proceeds to remove the tape from the boxes with surgical precision, as if he wants to avoid 'wounding' the cardboard. He then patiently flattens the boxes, piles them up neatly, and sets them aside. When he has collected a good number, he ties them together with blue plastic string in uniform packets and places one on top of the other, again with the utmost precision.

I'm mesmerised as I watch him. He's one of those people who conveys a real dedication to what they are doing.

Afterwards, he carefully places the uniform packets in the back of the three-wheeler. He handles them as if they were the most precious haul in the world. The end result is superb – I'm desperate to take a picture but I don't want to offend him. Finally, he gently lowers the lid back down over the bin, secures the packets, hops into the three-wheeler, turns off his parking lights, and eases out into the traffic, only to stop at the next bin a little further down the road.

I pause there for a moment to absorb what I've just witnessed. The guy does his job as if it were the most important in the world. Whether he enjoys it or not, he does it to perfection. He has truly inspired me.

I wish I could have filmed the scene to share it with my daughters, my friends and colleagues, and everyone in the world. The film would be called: 'How to Succeed'.

In the morning, wherever you're going, put on your best clothes. Love and honour what you do. But most of all, love and honour yourself.

Whatever you do, do it as if it is the most important thing in the world.

Be dedicated to what you do. Do it with passion and love. Whether you're a rubbish diver or a deep-sea diver. Most of all, do it for yourself, so that you can feel good about it and then, if you have to, worry about your co-workers or clients. Above all, try to leave the world a better place than you found it.

JUST LIKE THAT WELL-DRESSED MAN WITH THE SHINED SHOES.

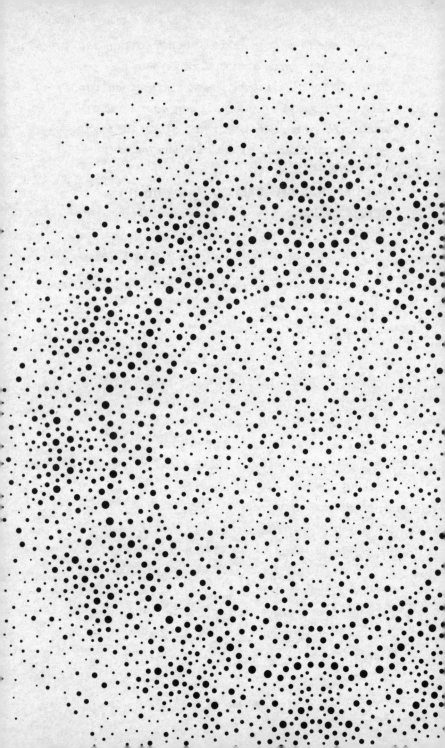

GREEK GENEROSITY

I WOULDN'T CALL HIM MY BEST BUDDY, but he's a good friend and I love and appreciate him, as he does me. I had some errands to run near his office in downtown Athens and so I gave him a call to see if I could drop by. He's an employee at a big, successful company. After greeting me enthusiastically and us both sitting for a bit in his office, he suggested we go for a cup of coffee nearby.

As we were leaving the office, and after talking to the person in charge, he picked out some company products to give me for my girls. I was surprised. It wasn't just one or two things; I couldn't help but think that the items he'd gifted me were probably what he was entitled to as an employee for his own child. In other words, he chose to gift my children what he could have given his own. At first, I said there was no way I could take them from him, but he insisted with that familiar Greek persistence springing from a deep need to share. He wouldn't take no for an answer. Deeply moved by his gesture, I thanked him warmly.

When we got to the café, he asked me what I wanted; he made it clear from the outset that he was buying. He told me to sit down and then went to order, delivering my coffee to me personally as if I was a guest in his home. We talked at length about what I was working on. He didn't just listen to me, he cared about what I was saying and gave me advice like a trusted business partner. When the bill arrived he refused to let me pay. 'Not on my turf!' he said. It wasn't the cost, but the gesture that moved me.

'Big deal!' you might say. But it was for me. I was deeply touched.

My friend was exhibiting Greek generosity. Those who've travelled know that you don't find such open-heartedness everywhere. They call it hospitality, but it's more than that; it's love – selfless love that gives, while asking for nothing in return.

A few years ago, a professor from England who had taught on our postgraduate programme was visiting. He told us a story I'll never forget. He was on holiday in Greece with his partner and they were in the picturesque Plaka downtown area, looking for a particular restaurant. They asked a local for directions. Not only did the man tell them how to get there, but he took them there himself. They thanked him and then noticed the man saying a few words to the restaurant owner. When they finished dinner and asked for the bill, the owner told them that the local had treated them to the wine they'd been drinking. The professor was stunned. He told us that he'd never experienced such kindness. Only in Greece. Concluding, the professor told us:

What you Greeks have is magnificent.
Don't ever lose it.

GENEROSITY WILL GET YOU FAR. EVERYONE COULD LEARN A LOT FROM THE GREEKS.

YOUR SHIT

IT ALL STARTED WITH THOSE RED CORRECTIONS the teacher made in our note-books in elementary school – she pressed down on the pen so hard that the lines went through to the next page. If your essay was a painting, red would be the main theme and your writing would be the background.

Growing up, it seemed as though those red marks became engraved on our brains. These red corrections are part of your life whether you like it or not. At first, they're your mother's corrections, then your teacher's, your boss's, and ultimately, your own. Accept them and you'll find peace. Love your mistakes and you'll be saved. You'll be complete only when you accept your mistakes – your 'dark side' as the experts sometimes call it. You could even call it your shit. Your shit is you and always will be, however much you may try to deny it. Manure is often scattered on top of the soil. In the beginning it smells, but then it becomes the best fertiliser.

We're all great during the good times, but your shit is the essence of life. To be truly comfortable with yourself, you need to learn to love your shit: to talk about it, share it, air it. Don't cover it up. Above all, own it.

The greatest people in the world became who they are because they accepted their shit.
It made them who they are.

Enough with the Facebook façade! Happy, shining faces everywhere, as if we're all Hollywood stars. Where's your shit? Where's your pain and anger? Where are your failures, vices, flaws, and inadequacies? They make you real. They are the things you can furnish your house with. Only then will your house be unique. Because it will reflect you.
Get real. You're here to love your shit.

   Christ said: 'Let anyone among you who is without sin be the first to throw a stone . . .'

THIS IS WHAT HE MUST'VE MEANT.

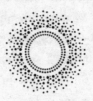

JOY

ONE OF MY FAVOURITE HABITS is waking up very early. As soon as I get out of bed, I go for a run. If I'm near the beach, I go for a swim afterwards, whatever the season. It rejuvenates me.

I take my habits with me wherever I go: my early mornings, my run, my swim, my breathing exercises, my meditation, writing in my journal, reading, doing good deeds, eating right, sharing – everything.

Yesterday, after my sacred morning routine, I was at the beach. Usually there's no one there so early in the morning, but not yesterday. There was a beautiful woman playing with the waves, the way my youngest daughter would play. She'd jump into the waves and ride along with them. As she faced the wind, her wet hair shimmering, she seemed joyful. I was mesmerised. At one point I heard a song, and I turned around to try to spot a radio. Nothing. Then I realised the woman was singing. She was playing with the waves and her whole being was immersed in her song. I dived into the water but when I emerged she was gone.

Today, my run lasted a little longer and I arrived at the beach later than usual. She was there again. She had finished her swim and she was wearing a bright, colourful sarong. She walked past me and we smiled at each other. I saw her features up close and, seeing the deep wrinkles on her face, I realised that this woman I had made out to be in her forties had to be in her sixties at least. I sat there watching her as she walked away and it seemed as if her footprints in the sand lit up one by one.

Joy is something within you.
You just need to find it.

Joy is like gold: the more you dig, the more you find. And it'll keep you young, happy, and strong. Just like the eternally young woman on the beach, who seemed to have found the fountain of youth. Drink that water and you'll conquer the world. As long as you are armed with love: for yourself, for others, and for life.

God wanted to hide a treasure so that man couldn't find it. At first, he thought to hide it at the top of the highest mountain. But man might get to the top of the highest mountain, he thought. Then he thought to hide it in the deepest part of the sea. But man might one day reach the deepest part of the sea, too, he reconsidered. I'll hide it at the centre of the Earth! Man will never reach it there. But something told him that man might get there as well. In the end, he found the solution. I'll hide it inside him, he said. He'll never think to look there.

THAT'S WHERE YOU SHOULD LOOK.

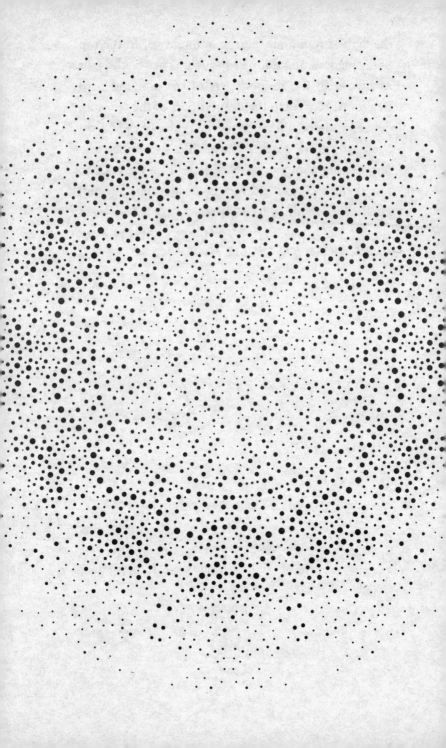

LOVE

THEY WERE SITTING BESIDE EACH OTHER a few tables away. It was midday and I was at my favourite diner. As they talked, they leaned closer into each other. It had been a while since I had seen that look. Gazing deep into her eyes, the guy gently grasped her neck, bringing her in even nearer. She didn't pull back. Their lips weren't touching, but they were so agonisingly close that you thought that, at any second, they would stick together like magnets. He played with her hair, combing it with his fingers, tucking a stray strand behind her ear, pushing her fringe to the side. His eyes were drunk with love and so were hers. I just couldn't help watching them, feeling happy for them, admiring them. After a while they left, arm in arm. Even the narrow pavement couldn't break them apart.

I kept thinking back to that gaze, the one that shoots sparks. It's called love and it will take you everywhere. It will connect you not only with your partner, but with everything. Love is the best spice

– it makes any food taste better. Love is the magnifying glass that concentrates the sun's rays to set light to any substance. It's the most powerful tool of all.

Love is what you feel for your work; it's the reason you get up in the morning; it's what fills you with gratitude for all the things you have and don't have. Love happens when you give thanks for a tasty plate of food; it's when you look at yourself in the mirror and like what you see. Love is what you feel for a stranger when you rush to help them out. Love is picking up that scrap of litter even if you didn't drop it. Love is saying a good word and delighting in it. Love is what you feel when you're doing your favourite hobby. Love is that sparkle effect in the movies when something magical happens. Only it's real.

Love is what makes the Earth turn.
Love is what will keep you forever young and happy.

Love is the reason you exist.

As I was sitting there, lost in thought, I saw a dignified elderly man with a cane, making his way with some difficulty up the steps to the diner. He was well dressed in a freshly ironed shirt and perfectly creased pants, hair slicked back. I recognised him: he was the owner, who had opened the diner fifty years ago. A day doesn't go by when he doesn't show up at his place. He has his own table, where he sits to take a breather. He set his cane against the chair and proudly looked round his establishment, eyes sparkling with joy.

I've seen that gaze before – the gaze that will take you anywhere.

IT'S CALLED LOVE.

HIGH SCORE

L ATELY I'VE BEEN TRAVELLING A LOT, attending self-improvement workshops so I can make my vision a reality: getting a class about personal values introduced into Greek kindergartens and elementary schools.

The more I explore these ideas, the clearer my vision becomes. To me, your life is your energy and the better you manage it, the better you are able to live. It's like those computer games where you get three cannons and each one is made up of lives. Every time you make a stupid move, you lose a life. When you lose all the lives, you lose that cannon. The good thing is that you can win lives and cannons back, as long as you play smart and follow the rules.

In life, there are two kinds of situations: the ones you can control and the ones you can't. Every time you waste time on the ones you can't control, you lose lives. Let's say you get on a plane. It's your job to plan your trip, choose the airline, book the ticket, and pack your suitcase. What the weather will be like, who the pilot is, and whether or not the plane crashes are none of your concern. Worrying about these things will only eat up lives.

Worrying about what other people think is none of your business either. All the assumptions you make and potential scenarios you dream up only waste your energy. Your job is to worry about what *you* think.

Any form of criticism or gossiping eats up lives, and lots of them. Whining, getting jealous or angry, feeling resentful and all the rest belong to the same group. It's like drinking poison and hoping the other person will die. You think you're just venting, but in the end this negativity brings you to your knees. Telling everyone your problems doesn't help you. Face your issues head on. Seek help from professionals if you need to. If you don't, sooner or later you'll wind up at the doctor's anyway.

Eating junk food, watching too much TV, not sleeping enough, spending too much time on social media, and telling the same old stories over and over all eat up lives. Griping about your mother, your boyfriend or girlfriend, and the President only eats up *your* lives – not mine or the President's.

Doing the same thing over and over again and not daring to take your life a step further slowly kills you, too. At first you don't see it, but at some point, you get to your forties or fifties and you're sick of yourself. Getting stuck in your routine is a slow, torturous death. Talent is there to be used and not stockpiled. If you don't put it to work, it becomes a huge, gnawing pain. At some point you'll discover you're missing a cannon and wonder who stole it from you.

Pointless dilemmas will also be the death of you. The other day, I overheard a conversation where a guy was praising the social responsibility programme of a particular TV channel. The woman he was with argued that there were lots of worthy initiatives that no one gets to hear about. They just went at it. What I don't get is why we have to choose when we can have both. We can welcome good deeds wherever they come from. Unhealthy preoccupations divide people. And they eat away at you.

On the flip side, there are simple things that pump up your energy and help you win back those cannons. They're things you usually don't notice or turn your nose up at: saying please and thank you; giving your seat up, especially when you don't know the person; planning a surprise for your best friend; helping someone on the street. And it doesn't matter if you don't have money. Say a good word. All these things are the children of love and they make you feel as if there truly is a reason you are here on this Earth. Because there is.

Smile even if you think that you have no reason to. Smile so that the reason will appear. Stand straight with your head high. You win lives that way. These lives don't show up at first but appear out of nowhere when you least expect it – it doesn't matter where from. That's someone else's job. Your job is to have faith.

Say no when you have to, and set boundaries. You don't win lives this way, but you manage to protect the ones you have. Care first about your opinion and later about the opinion of others. As children, we were told that this is impolite, but it's not: it's about protecting yourself. It's good for others, too, because they learn where they can stick their nose and where they can't.

Exercising, sports, and movement give you lots of lives. Motion is life. It keeps depression and too much self-reflection away and cleanses the mind and soul. Breathing right is also important – make sure to puff your belly out – that's the way to breathe correctly. Breathing deeply means you live deeply. And, of course, drink lots of water.

Focus on what you're doing and don't spread yourself too thinly. Remove all those distracting notifications from your mobile phone. If you concentrate all the energy of a laser on one spot, you'll bore a hole through the wall. That's the power of concentration. Those who did great things have one thing in common: they were aware of where to place their focus.

And there's another thing that gives you cannons right away. It's magical.

It's called gratitude.
Be grateful for everything.

Grateful for the job you have or don't have. Grateful for the children you have or don't have. You know how you love the whole world when you're a little bit drunk? It's like that, but without the alcohol. Be grateful especially if you have a warm bed at home and you're healthy. Everything else will fall into place – with actions and not wishful thinking. I read somewhere that health is the invisible crown on our heads and only those who don't have it can see it. So close your eyes and say infinite thank yous. You know the ones to thank.

Read every day and keep evolving and learning. Better to skip a meal than to skip reading. It's the oxygen of your soul and it will make your cannons sparkle.

Do all these things and your computer game will reward you by giving you infinite lives. That's why you're here: not for the 'game over'.

BUT FOR THE HIGH SCORE.

BE ON TIME

THE ENGLISH ARE KNOWN FOR THEIR PUNCTUALITY. I've lived in England, but the idea of being on time didn't sink in much while I was there. Even if I had three hours to get ready, I'd always be fifteen minutes late, to the minute. I was consistent in my inconsistency! I'm sure anyone I arranged to meet would add another quarter of an hour to our meeting time.

Many people had pointed this annoying trait out to me. But I was in my own little world. I thought they were being sticklers over nothing. And yet, how you handle the little things is how you handle the big things, too. It's a domino effect. If you're unreliable in your appointments, you're likely to be the same in your work. If you're unreliable in your work, this will be reflected in your personal relationships. If you're unreliable in your relationships, how can you rely on yourself? You just can't.

I see people who don't wear their seat belts when they're in the car, who don't charge their phones at night, who drive and talk on their phones without a hands-free, who eat on the run, who don't schedule in their commitments properly, who extend their limits like they extend their stomachs. You're essentially sending out a message as big as a billboard to yourself that says: you don't deserve all this, you jerk. You don't deserve reliability, money, and success. If you make discounts on the small stuff, then you'll do the same on the big stuff. That's how it is. Your store will have a huge discount sign in the window all year long and you'll wonder why the store next to you is always doing better.

My mentor used to tell me that the game is rigged *by* you *for* you. This is what he meant. You deal the cards and you get the hand. You're both the dealer and the gambler. So learn to control the cards better.

Learn to control your life better. Learn to control yourself better.

My younger daughter told me this, too. One night while we were brushing our teeth, she said, 'Daddy, I don't want to scratch my nose, but my right hand scratches my nose all by itself!'

Don't let your hand do whatever it wants.

YOU'RE NOT SIX YEARS OLD.

THE GREATS

WE WERE LISTENING TO THE SOUNDTRACK to the 1973 classic film *The Way We Were* and the conversation turned to Robert Redford: an outstanding actor and man. There's something magical about all his movies: *The Natural, Out of Africa, Brubaker, Indecent Proposal* – all of them. He's over eighty now, but he still makes for riveting viewing.

A friend of mine runs the Sundance Film Festival. He wants to help other people – budding filmmakers – achieve their goals, just like he has. He has a vision. He has passion. And he needs to share them.

Recently, I was watching the interview Nikos Galis gave during his induction to the Naismith Memorial Basketball Hall of Fame – he is a man of high ethics and few words. After all, he doesn't have to say much – he's a legendary figure both on and off the courts and probably the best European basketball player of all time. He stepped up to the podium, in his snow-white suit jacket and black bow tie, and gave an unforgettable, three-minute speech. He talked about a lady who approached him on the street in Thessaloniki. At first, he thought she wanted an autograph. Instead, she hugged him and thanked him for saving her son, who had been a drug addict up until Greece won the EuroBasket. Inspired by Galis, he quit to become a basketball player like him. 'This is the greatest gift that an athlete can offer to society,' he said modestly. He got a standing ovation.

Then, I thought about Giannis Antetokounmpo, another legendary basketball player, who recently signed a 100-million-dollar contract. Despite all the media attention, he hasn't changed. He keeps up with his daily practice and teaches lessons both on and off the courts. When the President of the United States talks about you and you continue to behave with the modesty and ethics you had when you were a young guy, you are indisputably one of the greats.

There are some people who are not merely good – they are one of the greats. Nobody asked them to do what they do. Nobody pushed them to aim so high. And you watch them keep at it; they're unstoppable. They keep looking for the next peak. They don't rest on their laurels. They want to share. They want to change the world, make it better. They don't do it for the money. They get money, but that's not why they do it. These people are the greats. You'll know who they are when you can't find words to describe them.

I was recently attending a workshop and the speaker showed us a video he had shot in a men's room in South Africa. The real star was the cleaner. As soon as the workshop speaker entered the men's room, the cleaner greeted him enthusiastically. 'Welcome to my office!' he said. 'A lot of people come in here every day,' he went on to say. 'I want them to leave happier than when they entered. It's my responsibility towards them. That's why I do my job as best I can. I scrub every grouting with the utmost care. I adore my work.' Grinning from ear to ear, he brimmed with pride. Even his eyes were smiling. By the end of the video my eyes had welled up with gratitude that such people existed. Such great people.

You aren't born great. You become great. It isn't about what you do, But *how* you do it.

JUST LIKE THAT AMAZING CLEANER IN THE MEN'S ROOM.

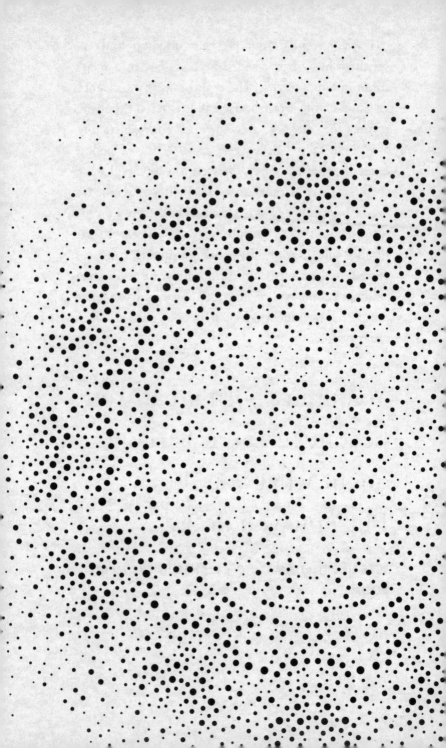

THE MOTH

IRIDESCENT, FRAGILE, EXQUISITE. At first, I could hardly make it out, but there it was, snowy white, on the bathroom window. Moths are sometimes called night-time butterflies and they are often even prettier than daytime ones.

There is no neutral act in the universe. Every act has an effect, be it positive or negative, and first and foremost it affects you from within.

Let's say you rent an apartment. The care you take of this apartment and the state it's in when you move out can receive a plus sign or a minus sign. If it's clean and there's no damage, that's a plus sign. If it's dirty and neglected, that's a minus sign. Add up those plus signs and your capital sum grows. But stack up those minus signs and they eat away at it. At some point you'll wonder, 'Where did my life go? Why did I fail? Who stole it from me?' Just think back to how you left that apartment . . .

You litter, you only look out for number one, you put your dreams on hold, you waste your life, you bad-mouth yourself, you stop evolving, you become judgemental, and you get addicted to social media, alcohol, gambling or TV, all adding to your liabilities.

You say a good word, you read, you discuss things with other people, you evolve, you dare, you break out of your comfort zone, you exercise, eat right, help out, you are a team player, you think positively, smile, believe in yourself, feed your leftovers to strays, empty your water bottle onto a dry bush . . . all assets.

When you act in this way, you can immediately feel the assets adding up. The same goes for the liabilities. You don't have to sit down and balance your accounts to know. You don't even need to check the register at the end of the workday. Deep down you know, before you even make that calculation.

You run a red light. You check and see that no traffic cop saw you and you are happy. Hold on a second! You know what you did and that's enough. You've added a minus sign to your liabilities, your self-worth, and self-esteem.

Don't live for others. Live for yourself.

I took a shower this morning. At one point, I saw the moth fluttering in the water. I had drenched it by mistake. I felt really bad. I got a paper towel to dry it off. I also put a little sugar there for it. I did whatever I could to save it. Plus sign! The moth finally made it.

Big deal. Is one less moth in the universe going to make a difference?

TO ME, IT DOES.

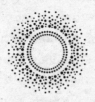

THE CONSTRUCTION CREW

IT'S 2005 AND WE'VE JUST MOVED into our new offices. My architect friend has created a great space. It's on the first floor of an office building and the ground floor is empty for the time being.

'Just keep your fingers crossed that no one rents out the ground floor,' he tells me. 'The noise from the construction crew will drive you nuts.'

'It's already been rented out,' I tell him. 'The crew starts remodelling in two months.'

'Uh-oh!' is his first reaction. Mine too.

'But wait, Mitsos. Let's check this guy out first. He might not be so bad,' I counter.

'No way. Lay down the ground rules from the outset. There's no way the crew won't make a racket. Make sure you insist they put in insulation first so you can work.'

'Hold on, Mitsos. Let's talk to him first.'

'Listen to me on this one. I know these guys. There's no talking to them. You have to show him who's boss.'

Before I even have time to go downstairs, the foreman comes up to meet me. Kostas is his name and he's all smiles. An honest, hard-working man. He's brought up some doughnuts from the bakery to welcome me to the building.

We start talking. We're on first-name terms from the beginning. I share my friend's concern with him.

'Don't worry, Stefanos! We're not doing any major work on the ground floor. The heavy stuff will be going on in the basement. You won't have any problems with the noise. And if you do, come talk to me.'

My friend's word 'insist' is running around my brain. I sweep it aside.

A year later, Kostas is one of the best people I know. The employees at the office all take their cars to his garage: he provides reasonable rates and top-notch work. He's more like a brother to me than a friend.

Don't assume things. Don't listen to that chatter in your brain. Every situation is different, unique. When you think you know something, you can often turn out to be wrong.

Don't assume.
Live life.

Get out of your cage. See the beauty, the love, the humanity all around you. Live free and let the bigger picture unfold. It'll reveal everything.

There's this guy in the waiting lounge at an airport, reading a newspaper. A woman is sitting next to him. He has a box of cookies by his side. Suddenly, the woman reaches over and helps herself to a cookie, without asking him. The guy gives her a sidelong glance but doesn't say anything. After a while, she takes another one. He still doesn't speak up, but he's starting to fume. And so it goes: he takes a cookie and then she takes a cookie. The guy is livid. It's down to the last cookie now. The lady has the gall to turn to him and ask, 'Do you want the last one or can I have it?' The guy grabs the box and stomps off, shaking with rage. He boards the plane and sits in his seat. He opens his bag to get his book out to try to calm down. And behold! There is his own box of cookies, untouched! All this time he had been eating the woman's cookies, and not only did she not say anything, but she offered him her last one.

REMEMBER WHAT HAPPENS WHEN YOU ASSUME. YOU MAKE AN <u>ASS</u> OF <u>U</u> AND <u>ME</u>.

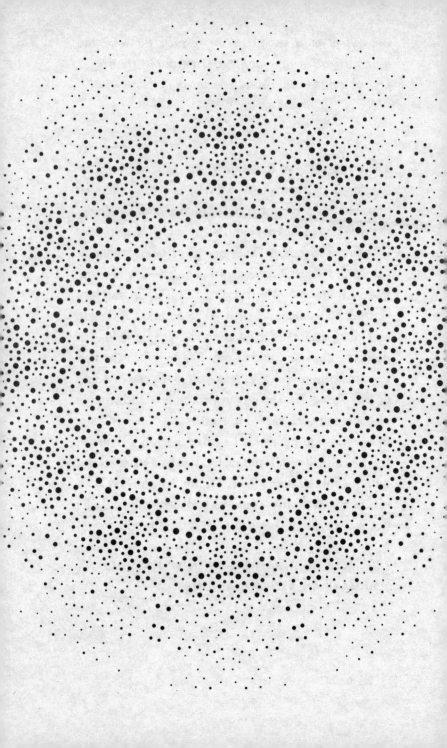

NEVER GIVE UP

YOU HAVE YOUR ISSUES. We all do. They're part of living. And you'll have them for as long as you live. What matters is what you do with them. That's what life is all about.

Some people just sit and look at their problems, in a positive way, admittedly. At some point, they'll go away, they say. But the damned things don't go away. Just thinking positively will not get you what you want. On the contrary, in the end it'll prove you wrong and disappoint you. Hope is merely the foundation. It won't raise the construction on its own. Been there; done that. I got an A+ in the hope department. It's in the action department where I got an F. It was the perfect recipe for let-downs, disappointment, depression, and illness.

Then there are those who struggle with their problems; and they struggle hard. They sweat it out in the gym of life for hours on end. They rage against the gym equipment, but those pull-up bars don't bend. And the more they refuse to bend, the more these people rage against them. For them, this life is a never-ending workout.

Others have long given up. They let the ship crash into the rocks. They allow their problems to pile up like heaps of dirty laundry on the floor. And for them, life is nothing but a dark dead end. Lots of anger here. But no question of trying to change things. I have a friend who belongs in this category. 'Let's go to a motivational workshop together,' I suggest to him one day.

'I'd rather die than go to one of those,' he replies. OK, then. It's your call.

Then there are others who have looked a little deeper. It's not all talk for them. They don't stop. They build. They always wonder what they could do better. They're not afraid of making mistakes. If they set the brick crooked, they'll take it out and put it back in straight. It's not the end of the world. Only if the cement hardens is it the end of the world. They also go to the gym but don't overdo it – half an hour a day is enough. These people love life and life loves them.

Whichever of the above categories you belong to, you have your own combination, just like a safe. One may have three numbers, another four, and another fourteen. Every time you find a number, the dial goes *click*. And while you're celebrating finding the number, you'll be inspired to look for the next one. And the more you seek, the more you'll find.

There were two seeds sown in the ground. 'I'm going to grow tall,' one said. 'I'm going to poke my head out of the soil and I'll make it. You'll see!' And it didn't stop. On the way, it came up against stones and twigs, but it kept on cheerfully and courageously. In the end, it made it.

'How long do I have to keep pushing upwards?' complained the other seed. 'Is there no end to all these stones and twigs in my way? Will these obstacles always be blocking me?' it grumbled. It rose, but it didn't put its heart into its climb. In the end, it grew tired. 'I can't take it anymore.' And it gave up – just one millimetre before emerging into the sun.

Never give up.

YOU NEVER KNOW IF YOU'RE JUST ONE LITTLE STONE AWAY FROM BREAKING THE SOIL AND EMERGING INTO THE SUNLIGHT.

GO THE EXTRA MILE

IT'S SEPTEMBER AND I'M ON THE AEGEAN ISLAND of Amorgos. As I am returning from a dip in the island's crystal-clear waters, I notice a sign for the monastery of Saint George Valsamitis. Something tells me to head there.

At first sight, the monastery is impressive: compact, sparkling clean, and as pretty as a doll's house. After paying my respects, I'm invited into the small reception room. The nuns treat me to a tall glass of ice-cold water and a Turkish delight. I notice a wonderful collection of icons on the walls. I ask who the painter is and am told that it's Mother Superior Irene, who also holds the services there. I can't wait to meet her. She's outside watering the flowers.

Mother Superior Irene is a relatively young woman whose bright eyes are filled with a lust for life, radiating energy and optimism. She tells me that she moved to Amorgos from Athens six years before, dropping everything when she laid eyes on the boarded-up monastery and fell in love with it. The monastery had been closed for 300 years and Mother Superior Irene had brought it back to life, turning it into a Heaven on Earth. She's planted thirty trees, and feeds more than twenty cats, which she's had neutered and vaccinated. She's a woman of action. She rolls up her sleeves at daybreak and stops only when it's time to turn in for the night. All day long, she looks after the monastery with tender loving care. Vivacious, active, capable, and cheerful, she is a true example to follow.

You see, there are some people who give their all to what they do, and then some. They are destined to be successful wherever they find themselves, be it in Greece, America, the Sahara Desert or on the moon. They can't help but succeed. Just like you can't stop the sun from rising.

They don't have a guiding star; they follow their own path. They have that itch that never lets them rest. They spring out of bed in the morning and can't wait to get to work, whether it's at the office or on a project of their own. Their mind is constantly coming up with new ideas. Something within them spills over that they need to share. If you ask them for 10, they give you 100, and if you ask for 100, they give you 1,000. When they bring joy to other people, they are even more joyful themselves.

It might be the taxi driver waiting to pick you up with a smile and a cold bottle of water, or the office worker who, even though he is earning minimum wage, works as if he's making top dollar, or the recycling collector who picks out the cardboard boxes and stacks them like an artist. What most people don't get is that these people don't do it for the praise or the money. They do it for themselves. It's their oxygen. Take it away from them and they die.

Why look for heroes when you can be your own hero?

FOLLOW YOUR DREAMS AND GIVE THEM EVERYTHING YOU'VE GOT. JUST LIKE MOTHER SUPERIOR IRENE.

SHARE

H E'S A GOOD FRIEND, though a rela-
tively new one. We haven't known each
other for more than ten years, but he's
already like a brother to me. For a while
now he's been complaining about lower-back pain,
so eventually, I convince him to start swimming, like
I do, all year long.

He called me the other day. He laughed before he
even said anything. 'Man, you know what? My back
pain is gone! Now my wife's started swimming as
well. She loves it. We swim together.' I was overjoyed.

I was encouraged to take up year-round swimming
and it changed my life, too.

This morning, when I went for my run, I saw ten
other people running. I always say good morning to
them. It's fun to see how they react. One guy eyed
me suspiciously and only when he was far enough
away did he return the greeting. A woman shouted
out her good mornings to me from way off. I had
joked around with another guy the day before – his
keys had been jangling in his pocket as he ran – and

today he motioned to me that he'd left them in the car. Another lady gave me the once over and finally allowed herself a hint of a smile.

Some runners laugh elegantly, as if they're having tea with the Queen, and some laugh out loud like there's no tomorrow. Some go in twos and I get a double dose of laughter. There's this other guy – I think he's English – who chuckles with reserve. I have a jokester who runs straight at me every morning and then swerves at the last minute. One day we're going to crash into each other, I'm sure. There's a whole spectrum of smiles and good mornings like the rainbow spectrum of my life.

If even one person tells you you've made a difference in their life, your life has been worth living.

Sharing is magical. You can share anything: an interesting book, a useful habit, a good word, a morning greeting, a smile. Share in someone else's pain when they need you. Delight in their happiness. Hugs, pats on the back, and holding hands are all part of the reason you're alive. Zig Ziglar, an American author and speaker, said, 'You can get everything in life you want if you just help enough other people get what they want.' He knew what he was talking about.

A few years ago, a speaker was visiting Greece. He was very important in his field of IT. He was also a morning person. Before dawn he had gone for a run at the Olympic Stadium in Athens. He shared with us how mesmerised he'd felt by the sunrise. He was happy, but he told us that, 'Something was still missing. I didn't have anyone to share it with. I wish my wife were here.' I remember that his eyes teared up.

SO DID OURS.

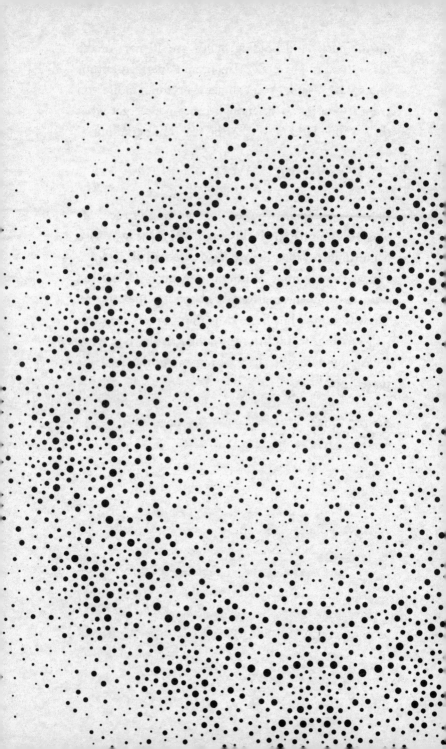

DON'T SPREAD YOURSELF
TOO THINLY

I PICK UP A VERY GOOD FRIEND OF MINE so we can run an errand together. We have to stop on the way to get a document from another mutual friend she hasn't seen in a long time. They are looking forward to catching up.

We are less than a minute from his place of work and her mobile rings. It keeps ringing as she rummages through her bag to find it. She finally locates it and tries to answer, but in her haste doesn't manage to swipe the green button fast enough. She finally gets it, but the other person has hung up. She's frustrated. She calls back, but the line is busy. Typical: the other person's also trying to call her. She hangs up. In a couple of seconds, she gets a text saying she had a call. She lets a few seconds go by and tries again. So does the other caller. They're both calling each other. Another text.

In the meantime, we've arrived at the friend's office. He comes out to welcome us and they give each other a warm hug. They start chatting. Just as the conversation gets going, her phone rings again. Same rigmarole: she tries to locate it in her bag, swipes the green button – a little easier this time. Meanwhile, her friend's waiting for her to finish. She hangs up quickly, but she's lost her train of thought. We try to find where we'd left off, but it's already time to go. She says goodbye. I can hardly contain my laughter about the whole fiasco.

Our mobile phones have this wonderful little setting called 'silent mode' and it's the most useful setting of all. If she'd used it after the phone first rang, she could have called that person back after she'd finished talking to the friend she was so excited to see, and everything would've been great. She would've been present in the moment. But she wasn't. It was as if she had poked a hole in her own balloon and there was no way to blow it up again. This is what we do, and this is how we miss out on both the big and the little things.

We haven't learned how to protect our focus and energy.

The greatest people in this world guard both of these with their life.

Another friend of mine, my very best friend in fact, loves deep-sea diving. He can go really deep under water. I've watched him as he dives. He glides through the water smoothly, like an eel. He doesn't push himself and make needless movements. He saves his focus and his energy. He saves his breath. And when he's in the deep of the sea, nothing else exists.

For me, this is the only way to live.

AS IF NOTHING ELSE EXISTS.

SHIPWRECKED

I WAS EXPECTING SOME VERY GOOD FRIENDS for dinner. In many ways, the three of us are quite different: different personalities, occupations, and world views. But in other ways we're also very similar: we feel things in the same way. It's what musicians call the harmony, and it makes all the difference.

The conversation got rolling straight away. Tonight, it was about luck: are those who succeed just plain lucky? Do they have their own secret rabbit's foot? Does luck even exist? Or do you create your own luck? And if you do, is it maybe only for the chosen few? Or is all this just hot air when you've hit rock bottom and your children are going hungry?

We split into two opposing sides. The two of us talked; the other listened and raised his objections; then we listened to him. The perfect conditions for a discussion to flourish. And flourish it did.

We said many things. In a nutshell:

You aren't born lucky. You create your luck when you work hard.

The hard knocks of life are a given. But the more curve balls you're thrown, the better. So, what's the secret then? Never give up. If you fall seven times, get back up eight times. And turn a deaf ear. Don't listen to those 'no's and 'don't's. Keep at it. Many of the greats, like Thomas Edison, Marie Curie, Walt Disney, Rosa Parks, Albert Einstein, Malala Yousafzai, and Steve Jobs, paid little attention to the naysayers.

However, there are plenty of good rules about getting ahead, even if you don't want to hear them. Just thinking about them can sometimes make your head spin. They say that you need to do something for 10,000 hours before you can be great at it. If you set aside three hours a day to practise, becoming a master will take you ten years. It's easier to blame everything on your lousy parents than to put in the work. Let's say you want to change a habit: maybe waking up early, working out, or reading. It takes at least sixty-six continuous days for your body to get used to it, for it to become second nature. And that's hard. So often we give up on the second day.

You really need to take risks. If you don't, you're done for. After all, you've got nothing to lose. And if it doesn't work out, you're still a winner because you've learned something. Love your mistakes; don't be afraid of them. They're all part of life's experiences.

Our conversation drew to a close with a quote from Nikos Kazantzakis's book, *The Saviours of God*: 'Our body is a ship that sails on deep blue waters. What is our goal? To be shipwrecked!'

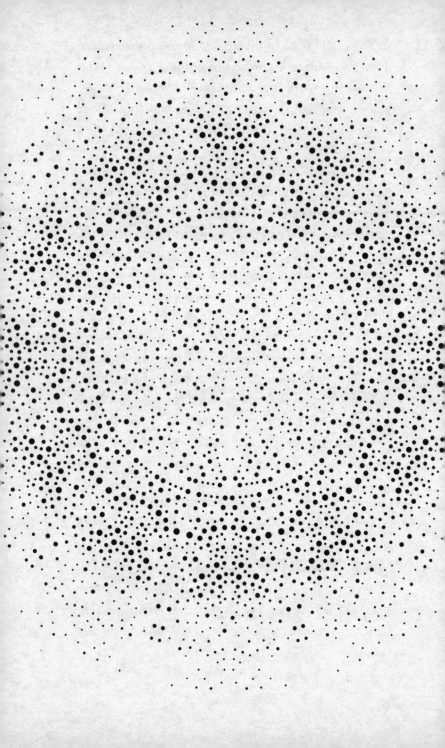

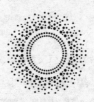

ONE MORNING ALONG THE SEAFRONT

I GOT UP EARLY THIS MORNING. I wasn't really in the mood to, but I'd made a commitment to myself to go for a run. I could've easily backed out. After all, I was going on my own. But I know by now that by committing to the little things, I'm ready to commit to the big ones, too.

I had said I'd run eight kilometres along the seafront. When I got to about six, I thought about quitting. Nobody would've been the wiser. But I didn't because I wanted to honour the commitment I had made to myself. In the end, not only did I do the eight kilometres I'd planned, but I continued for another 500 metres. I felt great that I'd kept my promise.

Along the route, there was road construction work going on, creating a big racket and lots of exhaust fumes. It annoyed me for a bit and I could have finished off my run in a bad mood. *Went for a run along the seafront and choked on the pollution!* But I focused on the sea, the sun, and the fresh air.

Wouldn't it have been a shame to let 100 metres ruin the remaining 7,900 for me? I didn't let them. Focus is key.

While I was running, I crossed paths with a like-able, middle-aged man walking at a brisk pace. I said good morning to him because I know how important it is to connect. I knew that this 'good morning' would make my day. And it did. He responded in kind and his 'good morning' rang out loud and clear. It came from the heart as did his smile. I thoroughly enjoyed it.

While I was running, I was listening to a podcast from *The Economist*. I always catch up on what's happening in the world while I run – two birds with one stone. It's very important to me to keep evolving and learning and I do it every day.

I finally arrived at the beach. That's where I hesi-tated. It was sunny, but the water was cold since it was the middle of winter. I paused, but finally took the plunge, literally and figuratively. I chose to be uncomfortable for a few seconds to feel better for the rest of the day because I knew a swim would rejuvenate me. We often choose the easy way out because we want to avoid discomfort, but that doesn't mean it's the right or the best way out. It often makes all the difference in terms of getting what we want.

I didn't always know all this. I didn't learn it at home or at school. I learned it as an adult after a lot of long, systematic work. It helped me change my life, though. As I kid, I remember always feeling I was lacking in some way, always waiting to be chosen and never choosing. There was always a 'Why?' hanging over my head. *Why was life so unfair to me?* I remember being unhappy often.

I suffered a lot during those years, but I didn't even realise I was suffering because my pain and I had merged into one being. Eventually, I found my way, and it changed my life. I'm not always in paradise; I often don't manage to achieve the things that I want to achieve. But even when I fall, I pick myself up, dust myself off and start all over again. And I learn from my mistakes. At night, when I look at myself in the mirror, I know I'm looking at a friend, not an enemy. 'Every problem is a gift', goes the saying. But most people throw them away before even opening them. I've learned to open life's gifts. There's another saying I like:

Don't wish for fewer problems.
Wish for more skills.

AND IT'S RIGHT.

THE MAGIC GLASSES

I DECIDED TO BUY SOME NEW SUNGLASSES because my old ones were falling apart. I tried to find the same kind, but they don't make them anymore. Though I'm a bit on the conservative side when it comes to eyewear, the optician managed to convince me to try some new, polarised ones. 'They're magic!' he said with a smile. After putting them on, we stepped outside so I could try them out. I can't lie, I could make out things that I couldn't see before.

Today I went to the airport to pick up the girls who had been away for a long weekend. I like to arrive early for some people watching. It was Sunday evening, and the arrival gate was crowded. Some people in business suits were waiting for clients holding A4 cards with names printed on them or written in marker. In front of me were two blonde girls – just like mine – whom I thought were twins, dressed in identical clothes. They were hanging on the dividing bar, half-swinging, half-balancing on it. They were playing, but every now and then one would 'accidentally' step on the other and they'd tussle, but they went right back to playing. A little further away, two cheerful guys were waiting, each holding a flower.

People of all kinds came through the arrivals gate: black and white, Greeks and foreigners, young and old, some alone and some in pairs, some with a devil-may-care attitude and some watchful, some smiling and others frowning. At one point, an odd character, who looked like a grumpy Smurf, came through. Another guy tried to go back through the automatic doors as soon as he'd passed through them and the security guard got very nervous. He brought the guy back through and tried to explain, in not very good English, what the rules were. It took a while for the guard to calm down. Just then, the mother of the 'twins' came through and the girls rushed into her arms. She knelt down and the three of them became one. 'Aww,' a woman next to me cooed. We exchanged glances and smiled. Next out was the couple the two guys with the flowers were waiting for. In fact, there were two more people in the welcoming party: the third was holding a card with the names of the couple on it and the fourth was filming the whole scene. The first two had pinned the roses to heart-shaped cards that had the pattern of the Greek flag and offered them to their friends, who burst out laughing. In seconds, the six of them were in a big group hug.

Then, it was my turn. My girls came out carrying huge paper aeroplanes and fell into my arms. It was our turn to become one. It had been three days since I'd seen them, and it felt like forever. They seemed to have grown and were even more beautiful. The hug was endless. My youngest broke the hug and asked me to carry her on my shoulders. 'No way!' I said and winked as I hoisted her up. Holding my ears like reins, she steered us out.

I'm really glad I bought those magic glasses.

THEY SHOWED ME THINGS I HADN'T NOTICED BEFORE.

TWO OF YOU

THERE ARE TWO OF YOU, NOT ONE. It took me years to get that. When I did, it changed my life.

I owe it to myself to tell this story, but for some reason I've been putting it on the back burner. I have a friend named Christina, who reminded me of it, thankfully. She called me the other day. She's someone I can have meaningful conversations with about ourselves, our children, and about life.

'You know why I called?' she asked me.

'Why?'

'I'm happy. I mean *really* happy. I called to tell you, because I know you'll understand. Stefanos, I've finally learned to give to my "self". I take my self for a walk every morning, just like I promised. Half an hour, early in the morning, and I charge my batteries. And they last the whole day. And listen to this! I also promised my self I'd go to a nice beach once a week. I sit there and empty my mind for a long time. I stare at all the blueness and let it seep right into me. I can't tell you how happy I am that I'm taking care of my self. I feel at one with it. I look at my self in the mirror and smile. As I've become happier in my self, my relationship with my husband and child has improved. I tell you, it's excellent.'

I listened, grinning from ear to ear and trying to breathe more softly so I didn't miss a word.

'I want to continue giving to my self every day. I've realised how precious I am. However much I give to my self, it gives back to me.'

You have another self within you. It took me years to realise that. People told me as much, but I didn't believe them. Your other self won't complain when things are going badly, but everything will start to get on your nerves. When your self is happy, it won't tell you, but you'll love everyone, like when you're tipsy, but without the alcohol.

Your life is your relationship with your self. And it's usually the most neglected relationship you have. We don't take care of our self. We bad-mouth it. We don't give it credit. Sometimes we are disgusted with it.

Imagine your self is your significant other. If you nagged at them all day long, what kind of relationship would that be? They'd have sent you packing long ago. That's what the self feels, too; only it doesn't have a way of dismissing you. You're stuck together. You've ripped your poor self to pieces, and it has no way of telling you. And it's upset; it gets depressed. Your poor self wants just one thing and it wants it from you.

It's called love.

Talk nicely to your self. Smile at it. Feed it well. Give it eight hours' rest each night. Buy it books to read. Take it for a walk. Walk with it. Exercise it. Sit with it. Listen to it. It has so much to tell you and it's so sad when every time it tries to open its mouth, you turn away to the TV, to social media, and to noise.

Love your self as if it was your child.

Take it into your arms and hold it tight. Cry with it. Maybe it needs a good cry.

It's nothing to be ashamed of; it's salvation.

There are two of you in there.

Get that into your head and your life will change. Sorry, I mean your *lives* will change.

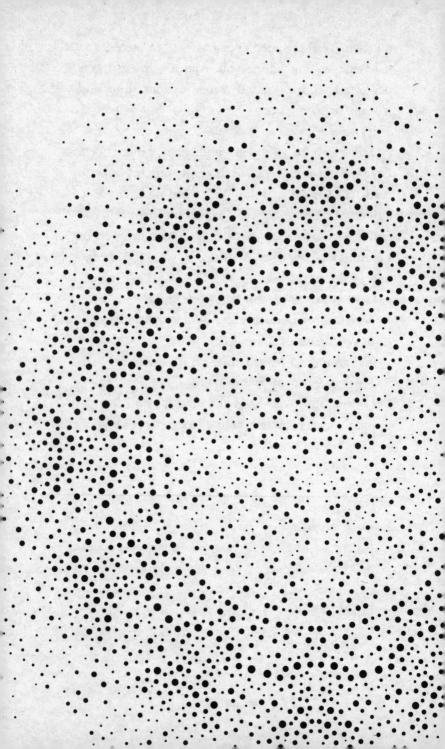

THE PHONE CALL

I HADN'T SPOKEN TO HER IN A WHILE and I was happy when I saw her name flash up on my phone.

'Hey! How are you?' I asked.

'I'm fine,' she says. 'But you! You've really lucked out!'

If there's one thing that irritates me, it's when people believe in luck.

'I haven't lucked out,' I told her. 'I've created my own luck. I've put in a lot of work.'

'Yeah, OK, but you've always had luck on your side.'

We chatted for a little while longer and then we hung up. I sat and thought about our conversation.

I didn't tell her I wake up every morning at 5 a.m. to build my life.

I didn't tell her I run for half an hour and then swim in the sea every day at the break of dawn all year round.

I didn't tell her I read one book every week.

I didn't tell her I watch inspiring online speeches

every day. I didn't tell her I haven't watched TV since 2001.

I didn't tell her how many weekends I missed spending time with my children to attend seminars.

I didn't tell her how many trips I've taken abroad, paying out of my own pocket, to listen to the best motivational speakers.

I didn't tell her how many years I've been doing group therapy to get to know myself and get in touch with my emotions.

I didn't tell her how many presentations I've arranged to give to educators all over Greece to make my vision a reality.

I didn't tell her how I watch my diet so I can be in good shape.

I didn't tell her how many miracle notebooks I've filled over the years.

I didn't tell her how many conversations I've had with friends and strangers to learn what I know.

I didn't tell her how much time I spend thinking about my goals.

I didn't tell her how many days and nights I've spent doing my breathing exercises and meditating.

I didn't tell how many affirmations I've made in the mirror even when I was tired.

I didn't tell her I will keep doing all these things till the day I die. There's a lot I didn't tell her.

Perhaps because they're only important to me.

It doesn't matter what your dreams are. What matters is how willing you are to make them come true. When the time comes for you to explain how you succeeded and how passionate you are about continuing, don't tell them what you did to get there.

JUST TELL THEM IT WASN'T A MATTER OF LUCK. TELL THEM YOU WORKED FOR IT.

TAKE IT EASY

H E'S BEEN MY DENTIST FOR YEARS and it so happened that our kids went to the same school. One day, while I was driving, I saw he had called me and I called him back. His assistant answered.

'Can I speak to Nikos, please?'

The assistant put the call through.

'Hey, Stefanos! I called because I heard that Sharma will be in London next week.' Robin Sharma is one of my favourite writers and Nikos knows how crazy I am about him.

'You're kidding, Nikos!' I was giddy with anticipation. He promised to send me an email with the details and I promised to send him the notes from Sharma's last workshop. We ended the conversation with a plan to go walking.

I love the traffic jams in Athens. I get to have some alone time, make some calls, and get ahead with my work.

Next, I call Eleni, one of my best pals. I like teasing her because she's so gullible.

She didn't recognise my voice at first. 'Who is this?'

'The author,' I say and we both crack up. We talk and tease each other. 'Some of us have to work at this time, you know,' she says towards the end of the call and she starts giggling again. We arrange to meet the following Saturday.

After the call, I get back to listening to my favourite speaker. This guy really makes me soar. In a while, I 'land' again in the crowded area of Pangrati. I have to sign some documents at the bank, which is on the main street. I park, buy a bottle of cold water from a kiosk, and enter the bank.

I find the person I need. She's efficient and polite. I sit down, give her my ID, and sign the document. 'You're good to go,' she says. It took less than two minutes.

'Already?' I ask.

'Already,' she responds with a smile.

For years now, I've decided to take life easy, not in the sense of living a life of ease, but of accepting things as they come. I like opening up and taking risks, even if the sea is deep and the waves rough. I love swimming in unknown waters now, but I do it without pushing myself. I take it easy. Lots of people think life is all about rowing upstream and I used to think so, too. But I decided to rid myself of that idea; since I decided to take life as it comes, I've found it's all become a lot easier. I smile at life and it smiles back at me. I embrace it and it embraces me. After all, everything is a mirror.

A smiling stranger waits for me in the glass cubicle of the safety exit to the bank with the door open. 'Do you want to go through with me?' he asks.

'Yes!' I reply with a smile. 'Do we fit?' I add, though it's clear we do.

'Of course we do!' he says. He's slim as well.

'Take care!' I say as we leave.

'You too!'

I get in the car, put my favourite speaker back on, and go on my way.

I am soaring again.

NICE AND EASY.

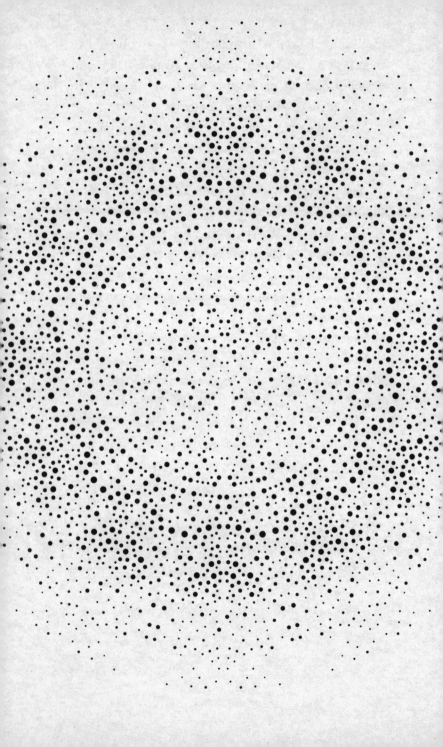

COMMITMENT

I HEARD THIS STORY AT ONE OF MY MENTOR'S WORKSHOPS.

Plato and Socrates are walking in the ancient Agora. Plato asks Socrates, 'How can I get what I want in life, Teacher?'

Socrates ignores him and continues walking. Plato asks him again. No answer. They arrive at a water fountain. All of a sudden, Socrates grabs Plato and plunges his head into the water. Plato is startled and tries to pull himself out, but Socrates holds him under. After a little while, he pulls his head out as Plato gasps for breath.

'Are you crazy, Teacher? I ask you how I can get what I want in life and you try to drown me?'

'When you need what you want in life as much as this breath you just took, then you'll get it,' the wise teacher told his student.

It takes commitment.

For some reason we so often quit when we're trying to reach our goals somewhere along the way.

We want the results but not the elbow grease that goes into getting there. We are in awe of Hollywood stars who have made it big, but these are people who gave their all for their dream, who put it above life itself, who never stopped trying regardless of the obstacles. We want to make an omelette without breaking any eggs.

Let me tell you this true story. When Steve Jobs, the founder of Apple, was eighteen, he was looking for a job. He went to the offices of Atari, which at the time was in its heyday. He told the receptionist he'd like to see the company president.

'Do you have an appointment?'

'No.'

'Then you can't see him.'

'I'm not leaving unless I see him. You'll have to carry me out,' Jobs responded with that (now) well-known sparkle in his eyes. The receptionist called the president's secretary.

'I have this crazy guy here who insists on seeing the president. He seems bright. If he has five minutes, I suggest he sees him.' After a while, the president met him and hired him, naturally. Jobs entered Atari that day hoping to get a job. He was determined. He didn't have a Plan B. That's what it means to be committed.

When you hear people say, 'I'll try', 'hopefully', 'I wish', and other lame stuff like that, don't buy into it. They won't do it. When you hear them say, 'I'll stop at nothing', and 'succeeding is a matter of life or death', then that's the person who will succeed. You can't cook an egg in lukewarm water; it has to be boiling. And your heart has to boil about your dream every day. And, of course, you have to get your arse in gear.

Then you'll be able to get what you want in life.

My girls know it, too. After telling them the Jobs story, I asked them, 'Do you understand what commitment means now, girls?'

'Yes, I do, I do!' said the little one.

'Tell me then.'

'Promise yourself you'll never give up.'

YOU GOT IT, HONEY!

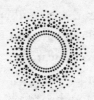

WRONG

I 'LL ALWAYS BE WRONG. Always. Me, you, and everybody.

At first, it sounds strange. But if you flip it around and look at it another way, you'll see that learning you are wrong is called evolution. We used to think the world was flat. It's not. Then we were told the world doesn't move, and yet it does.

Today you believe something. You might be sure about it. Sometimes you're even adamant. But you don't know today what you'll know tomorrow; what you'll learn, what will happen to you. Today, you don't know that you don't know. But tomorrow is your friend. It'll bring you knowledge, experience, and enlightenment. It'll overturn what you knew. Today you'll be more right than you were yesterday, but less right than you'll be tomorrow, and a lot less than you'll be the day after that. Is it a bad thing to be wrong?

Telling you you're wrong is the biggest gift people will ever give you, so don't look at them with contempt. Listen to them. Empty your mind so their ideas have room to fit. They might even pair up with your own ideas, but that's another story. Leave room for the new – it'll illuminate you, warm you, liberate you, and let you go forward.

I have this friend. When her sister got married, she was ready to blow her top because she was sure the groom was no good. All the rest of us thought he was a great guy, devoted to her sister, and was bound to make her happy. And he did. It took my friend years to see that for herself because it meant her prediction was wrong. She wanted to be right. We all do. But in the end she was happy for her sister, happier than anyone. I have this other friend. He endlessly complains about the political situation, his circumstances, work – everything! I used to suggest solutions. They were right under his nose and I wondered how he couldn't see them. Then I realised what was going on: he didn't want solutions. He wanted to be right. His problems were his toys. He was asking me to come play, not to find solutions.

Wanting to be right all the time makes you feel good at first, like a high.

But then you pay for it dearly.

When we were kids, we were taught to be right, to make sound arguments, to defend them, and have conviction. We were taught that being wrong is a weakness. We weren't taught to listen; we weren't taught that strong people are the ones who reconsider, who learn, and evolve.

One day, my mentor asked us:

'Do you want to be right or happy?'

YOU CHOOSE.

ONLY LOVE

GO TO BED EARLY. Your day starts the night before.

Before going to bed, plan the next day with pen and paper. Don't leave things to chance. Days turn into months and months, years. You only live once. Honour your life.

Wake up early. Really early. If your brain tells you to sleep in, don't listen to it.

Learn to negotiate with your brain to make sure you do what *you* want.

Go walking or running wherever you live for at least twenty minutes. It warms up your engine.

Listen to something while you exercise. You'll hear inspiring things from inspiring people.

Smile at the people you meet. Say good morning even if they don't respond.

They'll have their reasons.

Observe the beauty around you. It's everywhere.

Make a good breakfast.

Take a shower and enjoy it. Leave all your worries outside. Dress nicely.

Look at yourself in the mirror and smile. Talk kindly to yourself. You're the best friend you have.

Go to work in a good mood, even if you don't like your job. If you need to, then find yourself another job. But for as long as you're there, honour your work. That's how you honour yourself. Produce ten times more than you're being paid for, even if you don't earn a lot. You're doing it for you.

Have a mid-morning snack, like an apple or a banana. Come on, it's easy. Drink lots of water.

Breathe deeply. Puff out your belly even if it doesn't look very chic.

Take care of yourself like you are the most important person in the world. You are. They just didn't tell you.

Find fifteen minutes a day to read. Every day. Limit your time on social media. Don't turn on the TV.

It's a lie that you don't have time. You'll find it. Nobody will give it to you.

Dig deeper, ask questions. Don't think your beliefs are written in stone.

Take yourself out. Go to the movies or wherever you feel like going. You need to love and respect yourself. Your life is your relationship with yourself.

Write. It does you good. It soothes the soul.

Keep a journal and write down the beautiful moments of life. There are at least a hundred a day. Write them down. If you don't, they slip away. My mentor called them miracles. They are everywhere. Write them down. Don't let them pass by.

Write down your goals in a notebook and keep it updated. Revisit them and modify them. They're the compass of your life.

Spend time with yourself. Don't be afraid of it; it doesn't mean you're lonely. Not being able to be alone and always having to have the TV or the radio on isn't a good thing.

Keep good company, people who you aspire towards. Don't be afraid of them or envious. They'll take you higher and you'll become the kind of person you want to keep company with. Set your sights high.

Love thy neighbour, but first love yourself. You have no one else. Don't kid yourself: you come into this world and leave it alone. Without your children, your car, or your money.

Don't worry about what other people think. Listen to them, but first listen to yourself.

Don't gossip. Stick to your own business. The only person you can be in control of is yourself.

Always do good deeds. Help those around you, especially people you don't know. Your family isn't just your children. Everyone is your family. That's the only way you'll be happy. There's no other way.

Delight in others' happiness.

Don't believe in luck. You make your own luck. Understand that and your life will change.

Live your life to the fullest. When you laugh, really and truly laugh. When you cry, sob; when you hurt, feel all of your pain. You're not made of china. You won't break.

All the answers are within your heart and mind. Turn down the volume that emanates from outside. Turn off the noise and you will hear them. When they say God is within you, that's what they mean.

Use both your heart and mind. It's up to you to discover when to use one or the other, like a good chef who knows when to add salt and when to add pepper.

Evolve every day until your very last. Close your eyes and dream.

Only love fits in your baggage – the love you gave and the love you got. Only love exists.

ONLY LOVE.

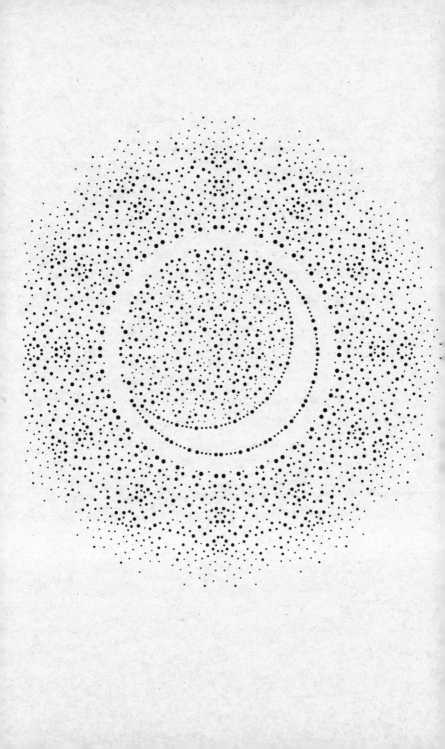